Compass Points for Riders

Snaffles

Carolyn Henderson

Compass Equestrian
Lond

Snaffles

Line illustrations by Maggie Raynor
Edited by Martin Diggle
Design by Hugh Johnson

British Library Cataloguing in Publication Data
A catalogue record for this book is available from the British Library

ISBN 1-900667-20-7

Published in Great Britain in 1997 by
Compass Equestrian Limited
Eardley House
4 Uxbridge Street
Farm Place
London W8 7SY

Printed in Egypt by
International Printing House, Cairo

CONTENTS

		Page
List of Illustrations of Snaffles		5
List of Other line drawings		8
1.	**WHY CHOOSE A SNAFFLE?**	9
	Skill, Knowledge and Choice	10
	Rules and Generalisations	11
2.	**STRAIGHT FROM THE HORSE'S MOUTH**	13
	Dental Care	13
	Conformation of the Mouth	15
	Handling the Mouth; The Lips; The Bars; The Tongue	
	Fitting a Snaffle	18
	Measuring a Snaffle; Checking Size and Fit	
	Snaffle or Bradoon?	20
3.	**HOW SNAFFLES WORK**	22
	Snaffle Action	22
	Riding Errors and Bitting Alternatives	24
4.	**MOUTHPIECES AND CHEEKPIECES**	27
	Which Mouthpiece?	27
	Unjointed Bits; Single-jointed Bits; Double-jointed and Multi-jointed Bits; Roller Snaffles	
	Mouthpiece Materials	32
	Stainless Steel; Nickel; Copper and Copper Alloys; Rubber; Nylon and Plastics	
	Cheekpieces	35
	Loose-ring Designs; Fixed Ring Designs	

5. GAGS, LEVER SNAFFLES AND LAST RESORTS   43
Gag Snaffles   43
Lever Snaffles   46
Last Resorts   47

6. BITTING YOUNGSTERS   48
When to Start   48
Which Bit to Use   49
Introducing a Bit   49

7. THE INFLUENCE OF NOSEBANDS   52
Uses and Abuses   52
Common Nosebands and Their Actions   54
The Flash; The Drop; The Grakle
Other Types of Noseband and Control   57
The Kineton; The Newmarket Bridle; The
Australian Cheeker

8. AUXILIARY AIDS AND BIT ACTION   61
Martingales   61
The Market Harborough   64
Bitting and Training Aids   65

9. PROBLEM-SOLVING WITH SNAFFLES   67
Preliminary Checks   67
Problems and Suggestions   68
Above the Bit; Behind the Bit; Bolting; Crossing
or Setting the Jaw; Leaning on the Bit; Rearing;
Becoming Strong; Tongue Evasions

Index   94

Illustrations of Snaffles

The snaffles referred to in this book are illustrated on pages 75–94 in the following order:

Bradoons (75)

Loose-ring bradoon
Eggbutt bradoon
Hanging bradoon
Loose-ring French link bradoon

Unjointed snaffles (76-78)

Straight bar flexible rubber loose-ring
Straight bar vulcanite loose-ring
Straight bar Happy Mouth loose-ring
Straight bar vulcanite eggbutt
Straight bar vulcanite full cheek
Mullen mouth stainless steel eggbutt
Mullen mouth Nathe loose-ring
Flexible rubber half-spoon
KK snaffle with port

Single-jointed snaffles (79-83)

Medium mouth flat loose-ring
Hollow mouth loose wire ring
Copper-coated loose-ring
Racing snaffle with large loose-rings
Wilson
Scorrier
Medium mouth eggbutt

Hollow mouth eggbutt
Loose-ring Fulmer
Hanging snaffle
Eggbutt full cheek
Half-spoon snaffle
Dexter ring bit
D-Ring racing snaffle
Jointed rubber D-ring

Double-jointed and multi-jointed snaffles (84-87)

French link loose-ring
French link eggbutt
French link copper eggbutt
French link hanging
French link full cheek
Dick Christian
KK schooling bit
Fillis snaffle
Dr Bristol eggbutt
Dr Bristol half-spoon
Dr Bristol D-ring
Waterford snaffle

Roller snaffles (88)

Magenis
Cherry roller snaffle
Single-jointed full cheek with copper and steel rollers
Single-jointed D-ring with copper and steel rollers

Gag snaffles (89-91)

Rubber jointed gag
Cheltenham gag with cord cheeks
Cherry roller gag with rolled leather cheeks
Single-jointed Continental gag (three-ring)
Continental gag (three-ring) Happy Mouth
French link Continental gag
American gag

'Last resorts' (92)

Twisted eggbutt snaffle
Chain snaffle
W-mouth

Training and handling bits (93-94)

Chifney
Stallion horseshoe cheek
Wire ring wooden mouth breaking bit with keys
Full cheek single-jointed breaking bit with keys

Other Line Drawings

	Page
Horse's jaw, showing location of wolf teeth	14
Measuring snaffle mouthpieces	19
Head carriage, hands and bit action	23
Alternating between a pelham and a snaffle	25
Measuring snaffle rings	35
The steering functions of racing-snaffle rings	36
A bitguard in place	37
A Wilson snaffle fitted	38
A Scorrier fitted	38
Using keepers with a full cheek snaffle	41
A loose-ring gag fitted	44
Polo pony in a gag snaffle	45
Options for rein attachments to a three-ring gag	47
The doubleback or cinch cavesson	53
The Flash noseband	55
The drop noseband	55
The Grakle noseband	56
The Kineton noseband	58
The Newmarket bridle	59
The Australian cheeker	60
Standing martingale	62
Running martingale, showing rings and rein stops	63
The Market Harborough	64
Bridging the reins	72
A tongue grid	74

WHY CHOOSE A SNAFFLE?

If you ask most riders which bit they prefer to use they will almost inevitably opt for a snaffle. Ask them why and they may come up with a host of good reasons — it is simple to use and fit; most horses go reasonably well in one type or another; it has the reputation of being kind on the horse's mouth. After all, to describe a horse as 'snaffle-mouthed' implies that he is a controllable and hopefully well-mannered ride.

The snaffle is the universal bit. Wherever you go, you will find that the majority of those who ride English style make it their first choice. In the right hands, a snaffle can be ideal: but, as this book will show, things are not always that simple. You have to decide which combination of mouthpiece and cheekpiece suits the conformation of your horse's mouth, gives the 'feel' that both horse and rider are happy with, and is applicable to his way of going.

It is often said that there is a key to every horse's mouth, but it may be more accurate to say that there is a key to every successful partnership. For instance, some riders may be happy with the way their horse goes in an eggbutt snaffle, while others may dislike the lack of mobility. If this means that the rider constantly 'niggles' at the horse, such a snaffle may not be the right one for that partnership.

If you have a schooling problem, which may range from a tendency to come above or behind the bit to full-blown brake failure, the right snaffle can help you to solve it. The choice of bit is, however, only part of the equation — the type of noseband, martingale or training aid you use can have a marked effect. So will everything else, from physical problems to the standard of your riding!

Skill, Knowledge and Choice

In order to be able to decide what sort of snaffle to use, you must be able to recognise when a horse is going in an acceptable way for his level of training, and when he is resisting. This may sound obvious, but a lot of riders seem to accept that their horses lean on the bit, pull, throw their heads around and so on as though these are actions they are powerless to change — or even part of normal behaviour. Every horse is going to resist occasionally, either because he does not understand what you are asking him to do or because he finds it difficult, but this should be a temporary setback rather than a permanent way of going.

The best way of learning what a well-schooled horse should feel like is to ride one. Unfortunately, this is easier said than done. True schoolmasters are hard to find and, unless you are lucky enough to find a teaching centre which offers lessons on well-schooled horses (a comparative rarity), you may sometimes feel that trying to progress is like attempting to swim against the tide.

While it possible to learn to work a horse on the bit if neither of you has reached that stage before, it is quite a difficult process. A patient and perceptive teacher is required — usually someone who can also ride your horse, so that it is not a case of the blind leading the blind. It is, however, much easier if you have had at least a few lessons on an established horse, so that you have experienced the feeling you are aiming for on a less experienced and/or less well-educated one. It is also important to ride as many horses as possible so that you can learn to recognise and overcome problems. Achieving a partnership with a horse who responds when you press the right buttons is only the beginning — you can then enjoy the challenge of the horse who does not understand where the buttons are!

Choosing the right kind of snaffle is often an important aid in solving problems. However, no bit can be viewed as a magic wand. You cannot expect to change from one bit to another and immediately find that your problems disappear — although you may sometimes see an instant improvement. Also, as horses have minds of their own, you may find that one snaffle does not provide a permanent answer. Some horses go better if you switch between two or three with similar actions: the slight differences between the bits seem to keep the horse guessing.

'Of every twenty bits I make, nineteen are for mens' heads and not more than one really for the horse's head' — Benjamin Latchford, loriner

Rules and Generalisations

Within these pages you will find information on all the types of snaffle currently available (and a few which, perhaps fortunately, are hard to find). Some are more common than others and a few may be of purely academic interest. However, this book is necessarily much more than just an illustrated directory. Bitting is a controversial subject with few hard and fast rules — mainly because horses cannot read. It is all too easy to decide that a certain bit will suit a certain horse, only to find that he disagrees! The intention of this book is, therefore, to provide a level of information that will stack the odds of making the right choice in your favour.

The old saying that 'all generalisations are false, including this one' applies as much to snaffles as to anything else. Too many guidelines about bitting have been propounded as hard and fast rules — for example, the frequently quoted advice that a thick mouthpiece is always milder than a thin one is not strictly true. It is always easier to view things in black and white, but in real life you have also to consider the various shades of grey.

That said, there *are* a few golden rules. These will be explained in more detail throughout the book but, whatever snaffle you are thinking of using, you should remember the following principles:

● The horse's mouth and teeth must be in good condition. He must be checked regularly by a specialist equine vet who appreciates the importance of dental care, or by a good equine dentist.

● The bit you use must be the right size for the horse, and correctly

11

adjusted. It should be chosen with reference to the shape of the individual horse's mouth and lips, inside and out.

● It must be well made and in good condition.

● Although all snaffles can be potentially mild or potentially strong, some allow more leeway than others for insensitive or uneducated hands. It is not just what you use that counts, but the way you use it.

● When you are educating a young horse, a simple snaffle of some kind is always the first choice. A horse can only work on the bit once he has learned to carry a rider and stay in balance, his muscles having developed through correct work to enable him to work from behind, with the back end as the 'engine'. A good outline comes from this process, not from using a curb bit or training aid to make the horse tuck in his nose.

There will be times when your choice of snaffle is slightly limited, notably when competing at the lower levels of dressage. The good news is that there is such a wide range of 'permitted bits' that you should be able to find a combination of bit and noseband that will enable you to work any horse comfortably and correctly in a confined space. If not, you have to ask whether you should really be competing at all and whether you might be better off going back to the drawing board for a while...

'The snaffle is a lovely bit, but it's the worst one on earth when misused' – Richard Maxwell, problem horse expert, trained and accredited by Monty Roberts

Later on, you may find that a snaffle is not always the best bit. For some horses and riders, in some situations, a bit with a curb action may give better results. A double bridle provides the ultimate communication between a skilled rider and a schooled horse, but should not be introduced until basic schooling has been established with a snaffle.

2

STRAIGHT FROM THE HORSE'S MOUTH

Dental Care

Before you even start thinking about what type of snaffle to use, it is essential to make sure that your horse's mouth and teeth are in good condition. This is equally important whether you are dealing with a youngster who is about to be introduced to a bit for the first time, a top-class competition horse, or a happy hacker. If a horse is uncomfortable, he will resist any bit.

Do not underestimate the far-reaching effects of bitting problems. A leading chiropractor says that, if a horse has a problem which makes him tilt his head, he will hold himself out of alignment to try to alleviate the discomfort, and may consequentially set up problems in other parts of his body.

By the same token, you have to remember that not all problems which manifest themselves in resistance to the bit actually start in the mouth. A horse may be 'mouthy' because he finds the work you are asking him to do is difficult; because his saddle fits badly and causes discomfort; or even because he has a hind limb problem. So, while dental problems must always be ruled out first, solutions may not always be so clear-cut as you might like.

Horses change their teeth between birth and four-and-a-half to five years. During that period they should be checked and, if necessary, attended to twice a year. After that, some animals may be fine with annual checks while others will still need attention every six months. The best person to do the work is either a specialist equine vet with a good knowledge of dental work, or a qualified practitioner registered with the Worldwide Association of Equine Dentistry.

The commonest problems are sharp edges on the molars, retained caps in young horses and wolf teeth. Sharp edges can be rasped or floated and caps (temporary teeth that do not always fall out when replaced by permanent ones) can be removed. Wolf teeth (shallow-rooted teeth in front of the pre-molars, that can be found in the upper and lower jaws) are best removed as they can interfere with the action of the bit.

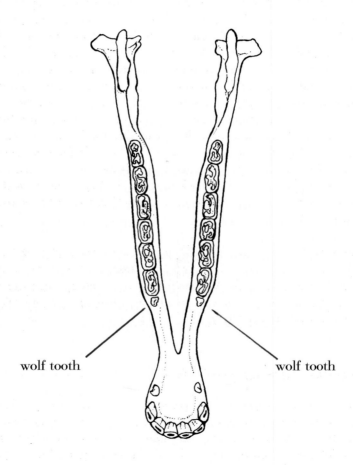

wolf tooth   wolf tooth

Horse's jaw, showing location of wolf teeth

Signs that a horse needs his teeth seeing to include resistance to the rider, a reluctance to take the bit when bridled, and quidding (dropping bits of food out of his mouth when eating). Dental care is an investment; not only will you have a happier horse, you will also save money on feed. A horse who cannot chew properly will not digest his food efficiently, which can lead to everything from bigger feed bills to colic.

Most equine dentists say that a proper examination can only be made if a dental gag is used. This holds the horse's mouth open so that the dentist can see and feel inside the mouth safely. Some people believe that they can assess the state of a horse's teeth by taking hold of the tongue, holding it out to one side of the mouth and feeling the edges of the teeth, but this is neither very thorough nor very safe — if a horse closes his mouth on their fingers they may soon be counting to four instead of five. Gary Singh-Khakhian, equine dentist and former president of the Worldwide Association of Equine Dentistry, suggests running your fingers down the sides of the horse's face in line with the bridle cheeks and applying gentle pressure. If the horse shows signs of discomfort, such as throwing up his head, he needs a dental check-up — but even if he does not, such checks should be part of his routine.

'Unfortunately, we do our formative work with horses at a time when their mouths are in a constant state of change. This is particularly true of Flat racehorses, who are broken as yearlings and expected to be at their peak as two- and three-year-olds' — Gary Singh-Khakhian, Master Equine Dentist.

Conformation of the Mouth

Everyone knows the importance of conformation in relation to a horse's athletic ability, but there is one aspect which is often forgotten. The shape of his mouth and tongue can have an important effect on the type of snaffle you choose, and may mean that some of the oft-quoted generalisations on the severity or otherwise of mouthpieces do not apply.

Handling the mouth

Many horses are reluctant to have their mouths handled and have to be taught that this is not necessarily unpleasant. Try rubbing the upper and lower gums gently with your forefinger, a technique familiar to devotees of the Canadian equine awareness expert Linda Tellington-Jones. (Linda says that this also helps prepare a young horse for being bitted.) Gentle finger pressure on the bars of the mouth will persuade most horses to open their mouths but, if this does not work, try tickling the tongue. With practice and gentle handling the horse will learn to co-operate — but you still need to be careful where you put your fingers.

The lips

Starting from the outside and working in, look at your horse's lips. Are they fleshy or thin? Fleshy lips will mean that a correctly adjusted snaffle will wrinkle the corners of the mouth, but thin lips will be pulled uncomfortably high in the corners if you produce wrinkles. Are the lips supple and in good condition, or do they have cracks or sores, particularly in the corners? Such injuries can be caused by a badly fitting or badly made bit, or by using one with saliva and/or food encrusted on the mouthpiece.

The bars

Next, look at the nature and condition of the bars of the mouth, where the bit rests. Thoroughbreds and horses with a lot of Thoroughbred blood often have a thinner layer of skin over the bars than those who are more cold-blooded. Occasionally you may find scar tissue, which means that the horse pulls against his rider or has been ridden by someone with rough hands — more often than not, the two go together. Scar tissue inevitably lessens the sensitivity of the mouth, but you may regain some of it by correct schooling and using a snaffle which acts in a slightly different way from the bit which caused the problem.

The tongue

The shape and size of the horse's tongue have a bearing on which mouthpieces he will find comfortable. It does not matter whether the tongue is large or small, so long as it corresponds to the size of the lower jaw (which is naturally narrower than the upper jaw). A relatively large tongue will be more susceptible than normal to pressure from a jointed bit (see below), and may also make it difficult for the horse to close his mouth, which can lead to a drier mouth than is ideal. If the mouth is kept lubricated with saliva, the bit will slide over the tongue and bars, but if the mouth is dry, it may drag at the skin and cause soreness. Some bits are designed to encourage salivation — see *Which Mouthpiece* and *Mouthpiece Materials* in Chapter 4.

Because the tongue acts as a cushion between the bit and the bars, a very narrow tongue may not be so effective as a 'normal' one. In this case, a mouthpiece such as a Nathe or Happy Mouth (*see page 34*) may be more comfortable for the horse. If he draws back his tongue or manages to put it over the bit, he will also make life more uncomfortable for himself, so you will have to persuade him that this is not a good idea —see *Tongue Evasions* in Chapter 9.

All snaffles put pressure on the tongue to a greater or lesser degree. While some horses respond positively to tongue pressure, others hate it so, if your horse comes into the latter category, you will have to choose your snaffle accordingly. He, along with the horse who has a fleshy tongue, will often prefer a French link snaffle to a single-jointed one (see *Which Mouthpiece* in Chapter 4). This is because the outside edges of the tongue, being thinner than the centre, will also be more sensitive to pressure.

In theory, because it has a greater bearing surface, a bit with a thick mouthpiece has a potentially milder action than one with a narrow mouthpiece. However, if the shape of a horse's mouth is such that he cannot close it around a thick mouthpiece, he may well find a thinner one much more comfortable

One of the most interesting developments of the past few years is a German-made range of snaffles called KK, now widely distributed. These, according to the manufacturers, 'have been specially adapted to suit the anatomy of the horse's mouth and are gentle on the sensitive edges around the tongue'. The idea behind these bits, which have shapes rather different from conventional snaffles, is that when contact is established through the reins, pressure is shifted from the edges to the centre of the tongue. John Patterson bits follow the same school of thought: the mouthpiece arms are curved to follow the shape of the horse's mouth.

Fitting a Snaffle

In order for the horse to be comfortable, the bit must be the correct size and be adjusted at the right height. Many people use bits with mouthpieces that are too long: with a single- or double-jointed bit, this means that it hangs too low in the mouth and the horse may try to put his tongue over it. This may not be quite such a problem with a mullen mouthed (slightly arched) or straight bar bit, but — as with jointed mouthpieces — there will still be too much side-to-side movement and the bit's cheeks will bang against the horse's lips and teeth.

A bit that is too short will also cause problems. The cheekpieces will pinch the lips, pressing them against the horse's teeth and perhaps causing sores both inside and outside the mouth. Pinching is even more likely if you use a loose-ring snaffle that is too small, since the lips can become trapped between the loose-ring and the holes in the mouthpiece through which they turn.

Measuring a snaffle

To measure a bit, put it on a flat surface so that the mouthpiece is fully extended and measure from A to B. British bit manufacturers used to measure in increments of half an inch; some makers and retailers still stick to the imperial system, but others have gone metric.

Either way, horses, like people, are not necessarily made in perfect half-inch or centimetre increments, so you might have to try different makes and both measuring systems to get the perfect fit. (At one time, mouthpieces were made in quarter-inch gradings. Although some manufacturers still do this, many retailers nowadays do not want to stock so many sizes. However, a good retailer will usually be willing to order a special size for you.)

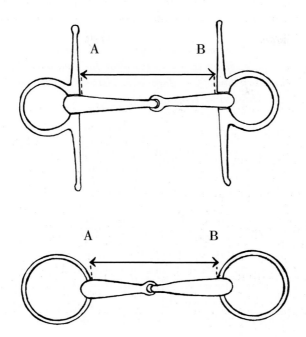

Measuring snaffle mouthpieces

Checking size and fit

To judge whether a snaffle is the correct size for a particular horse, adjust the height of the bridle cheekpieces so that the bit fits snugly into the corners of the mouth — taking account of the shape of the horse's lips, as discussed earlier. A mullen or straight bar bit can be slightly lower than a jointed one, if the horse finds it more comfortable, but it must never drop down too far.

It is impossible, in abstract, to give an absolute ruling on what constitutes ideal fit for an individual horse/rider partnership. The best advice is to go 'by the book' to start with, but to remember that some

19

horses have particular preferences. Altering the fit by just one hole on one cheekpiece can sometimes make a lot of difference, but if you do adjust on one side only, remember to even up the bit gently in the horse's mouth so that it is not lopsided.

'If a horse tends to lean on the bit, it can sometimes help to raise the bit by one hole. If he tends to go with his head too high, lowering it by one hole may help.' — Jennie Loriston-Clarke, *former international dressage rider and trainer.*

When the bit is at the right height, put a thumb in each ring and extend the mouthpiece slightly (if it is jointed) so that it is straight in the horse's mouth. You should be able to fit the width of an adult's little finger (about half an inch or 12mm) between the bit and the horse's lips on each side. Again, you have to take into account whether the horse has thin or fleshy lips, but there should not be more space than this on each side. If the bit has fixed cheeks — full cheek, egg-butt or D-ring — you may need slightly less space between the bit cheeks and the horse's lips than if it has loose-rings. This is because there is more danger of a loose-ring bit pinching. An alternative is to use rubber bitguards to remove the risk: some people may find them unsightly, but they help to prevent discomfort and to keep the bit stable (*see pages 36–7*).

In addition to checking that the bit is of correct size, make sure that it is well made. Look for a smooth finish, with no rough edges which could cause discomfort. Also, check that the bit is symmetrical — you may occasionally find a jointed bit where one arm of the mouthpiece is significantly longer than the other. This means that pressure will be uneven, which may lead to problems and resistances.

Snaffle or Bradoon?

Animals whose mouths are too small to accommodate thick mouthpieces often go well in a bradoon. A bradoon (sometimes called a bridoon, though purists insist that the first term is the correct one) is a thin, lightweight snaffle that is used in conjunction with a curb bit to make a double bridle. You may sometimes hear the bits for a double bridle described as a Weymouth set, after a type of curb called a Weymouth. At one time there were many kinds of curb, all with different names.

Bradoons also offer many variations in mouthpieces and cheek-pieces: single-jointed, double-jointed, loose-ring, eggbutt, hanging cheek and so on. Although designed to be half of a partnership, they suit some horses and ponies very well when used alone. Because the mouthpieces are thin, they have a smaller bearing surface than ordinary snaffles and some people class them as severe. However, this is theoretical and, if used correctly in the correct context, they are no more severe than snaffles with thick mouthpieces. The only potential disadvantage is that the bit rings are much smaller than those on standard snaffles. If there is a risk that these might pinch or slip through the horse's mouth, the bradoon can be used with rubber bit-guards although these are unfortunately not permitted in dressage tests.

'There is so much you can do with a snaffle... Whatever the resistance – upwards, downwards, to the right or the left – in the snaffle you have the wherewithall to overcome it. However, in order to act only on the resistances, you must never use your hands towards your body, never use a backward action, since this would have an adverse effect on the horse's impulsion and even its balance... The snaffle is such a fine thing!' *François Baucher (1796 - 1873).*

HOW SNAFFLES WORK

In order to understand how a snaffle works it is necessary to consider much more than the type of bit at the end of the reins. You also have to take account of the stage of the horse's schooling, the rider's use of the aids — and this means all of them, not just the rein aids — and the way in which a particular noseband, martingale or training aid comes into effect.

Snaffle Action

To say that a snaffle has a raising action and a curb bit has a lowering one is too simplistic. If the rider's hands are carried correctly, rein aids will produce upward pressure on the corners of the mouth, but that is not the same thing as raising the head. In fact, talking about the bit having a dominant effect on head carriage is treading on dangerous ground, because head carriage ultimately depends on whether or not the horse is working from behind.

When a horse is first backed and ridden, he is very likely to be on his forehand because he has to get used to the weight of the rider and learn to adjust his centre of gravity. At this stage of training the snaffle will have a distinct upward action, and will usually act more on the corners of the mouth than on the bars. As the horse finds his balance and learns to work from behind, with his hocks underneath him, his head carriage will become higher and nearer to the vertical. The rider will still be aiming to keep a straight line from the bit rings through the hands to the elbows – not because it looks nice, but because it is the best position in which to give a sympathetic and consistent 'feel'.

In consequence, the angle of the rider's elbows will usually (depending on the human and equine anatomy) be more closed. Therefore, in general, the more advanced the horse becomes in his work and the more collected his outline, the more the snaffle will act on the bars as well as the corners of his mouth. The type of mouthpiece and cheekpieces will also play a part – for instance, a D-ring snaffle will tend to act in more of an upwards fashion than a loose-ring, while a hanging snaffle will have a definite action on the poll.

The horse's head carriage, the rider's hands and bit action

a) pressure on the corners of the mouth

b) pressure on the bars of the mouth

Riding Errors and Bitting Alternatives

All sorts of problems arise when riders try to lower the horse's head through rein aids alone — usually by lowering their hands and wiggling at the bit. What happens is that the horse sets his jaw against the rider's hands and either raises his head still further, or else tucks in his nose to try to get away from the discomfort. The latter evasion may fool an inexperienced rider into thinking that the horse is now on the bit, whereas, in fact, he is not working through from behind.

We often talk in terms of horses having 'snaffle mouths', but perhaps we should also think of riders having 'snaffle hands'. One of the greatest compliments you can pay a rider is to say that he or she has 'light' or 'good' hands, but you cannot truly have good hands unless you have a balanced, independent seat, entirely independent of the reins. A rider who has not yet achieved an independent seat may attempt to offer a light contact, but will not be able to guarantee or sustain it — this is not the same thing as light hands.

A horse who understands what is being asked of him, who has been schooled to work from behind and has no physical problems which make him uncomfortable in his mouth, will usually work nicely in some sort of snaffle if ridden correctly. This scenario can change if, for example, horse and rider are put in a more exciting or demanding situation, or if you have a very large and/or powerful horse with a small rider. You may also observe a communication breakdown if a nervous rider, teamed with a sensitive, forward-going horse, tries to slow him down predominantly through rein aids (see *Becoming Strong* in Chapter 9). Unfortunately, it is all too easy for a tense rider to set up a vicious circle by pulling or fiddling with the reins in an attempt either to slow down an onward-bound horse or to produce an 'outline'. This circle can sometimes be broken by substituting a pelham with two reins for a snaffle. The rider must be taught to use the top and bottom rein independently, and the curb chain must be fitted correctly.

Some experts may frown on this, but it is a substitution that others — including some leading teachers whose methods are based on classical principles – use successfully.

There are several reasons why a partnership may be happier with a pelham than a snaffle. Often, horses who naturally tend to pull or yaw in a snaffle will go kindly in a mullen mouth pelham, which can have a variety of mouthpieces. (The most common ones are stainless steel, metal incorporating copper, flexible rubber and vulcanised rubber — see *Mouthpiece Materials* in Chapter 4.) Also, if a rider thinks he or she has more control in a pelham and stops grabbing at the reins, the horse no longer feels uncomfortable or restricted and both

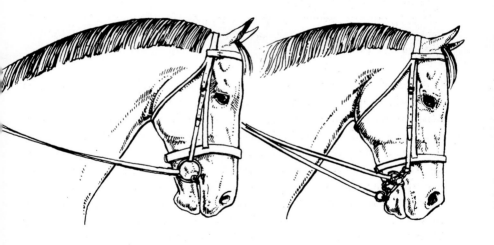

Alternating between a pelham and a snaffle

parties become more relaxed.

Another reason for trying a pelham is that it may suit the horse's conformation better than a snaffle; in particular, better than a jointed snaffle. Horses and ponies with short mouths, especially those who also have short, thick necks, often go well in pelhams. This applies to cobs and to some native ponies (who do not, of course, necessarily have short or thick necks!).

Once the rapport between horse and rider has been established, it may be possible to go back to a snaffle, or to alternate between a snaffle and a pelham. If a horse goes well in a vulcanite mullen mouth pelham, he may work well on the flat in a snaffle with the same mouthpiece. This sort of lateral thinking is useful for horses who go better in pelhams, but whose riders are limited to the permitted snaffles when taking part in dressage competitions

4

MOUTHPIECES AND CHEEKPIECES

There are so many different types of snaffle that you could never expect to find them all in one shop. Manufacturers' catalogues always make fascinating reading, and every time you think that there cannot possibly be any more permutations of mouthpieces and cheekpieces, someone comes up with a new idea. Whether they are all good ideas or not is another matter; fashion plays a large part in the equipment we use, and if a top rider seems to get good results by using a certain type of bit, then a lot of people are encouraged to see if it works for them.

Which Mouthpiece?

The designs of both mouthpiece and cheekpiece have to be looked at together, as they determine the angle at which the mouthpiece rests, whether the bit tends to stay still in the mouth or to make continual small movements, and whether there is pressure on the side of the face. However, since it is the mouthpiece which is the basis of the bit's action, while the cheekpieces enhance or refine this, it makes sense to start by looking at the design of the mouthpiece and the materials from which it can be made. The traditional basic designs are straight bar, mullen mouth, single-jointed, double-jointed and designs with rollers set in or around them.

Unjointed bits

The straight bar snaffle — unlike the mullen mouthed or 'half-moon' one — does not allow room for the tongue, and therefore applies more tongue pressure when contact is taken on the reins. Perhaps for this reason, it is not so popular as it used to be, and is now used more as an in-hand bit than for riding.

The mullen mouthpiece provides some tongue pressure, but because of the slight arch this is not so definite as that of a straight bar. Many riders do not like it, believing that it does not have the flexibility of 'feel' offered by a mouthpiece with one or more joints, but some horses and ponies like it. Because it does not drop down in the centre like a jointed snaffle, it can be a useful option for a horse who tries to put his tongue over the bit even though obvious causes of this have been eliminated (see Tongue Evasions in Chapter 9). For this reason, some trainers like to use it on horses who are just starting their training. Not surprisingly, young horses often do not understand why they suddenly have a piece of metal or rubber in their mouths, and will attempt to spit it out. Alternatively, if the bit is too low, a youngster may try to put his tongue over it. A mullen mouth snaffle can be fitted high enough in the mouth to prevent this without pulling up the corners of the lips too far, as is the risk with a single-jointed bit.

KK schooling and correction bits fall into the unjointed category, but stand alone through their design and purpose. The schooling bit is designed to provide a transition between a jointed snaffle, such as the double-jointed training bit from the same range, and a double bridle: it is also said to help with the horse who tries to put his tongue over the bit. The correction bit is aimed at strong horses and pullers, but is designed to work without exerting massive leverage (see *Becoming Strong* in Chapter 9).

Single-jointed bits

The single-jointed snaffle is the one most commonly used, although if you asked a hundred riders why they used it, a large percentage would probably have no logical answer other than that it was the bit in which the horse was ridden when they bought him. In one way this is a perfectly acceptable response, as there is no reason to change a bit with which both horse and rider are happy. On the other hand, it is a shame that more riders are not aware of the improvements that can be made to their horses' comfort and way of going by, for instance, simply changing a single-jointed snaffle for one which suits him better, such as a double-jointed French link.

Of course, there is nothing wrong with a single-jointed snaffle if the horse goes well in it, and many do. There have been many discussions amongst learned people about whether a single-jointed bit is more or less severe than one with two joints, and opinions vary. One way of looking at the issue is that severity does not really come into it, because that depends largely on how the bit is used. If a horse goes better in a single-jointed snaffle than a double-jointed one, then the former should be the first choice, and vice versa.

The design of the single-jointed snaffle is such that it allows room for the tongue and has a squeezing, or nutcracker, action. If the arms of the mouthpiece are straight, the nutcracker action will be sharper than if they are shaped. It is important to check that the mouthpiece arms are the same length, as if one is much longer than the other the supposedly central link will be off-centre, so more pressure will be put on one side of the mouth than the other. This should not happen with bits supplied by reputable manufacturers with plenty of 'horse sense', but one major manufacturer says that, at every international trade fair, would-be competitors surreptitiously take photographs of their bits and then try to copy them — often producing asymmetrical bits with rough edges.

It is particularly important that a single-jointed snaffle is the correct size and is correctly adjusted. If it is too big or too low, the central joint will hang too low in the horse's mouth. Fulmer and full cheek snaffles (see next section on cheekpieces) are designed to be used with small leather keepers which attach the bit cheeks to the bridle cheekpieces and keep the mouthpiece at the theoretically correct angle in the horse's mouth. This has the added advantage of ensuring the mouthpiece does not drop too low. However, some horses go better if full cheek snaffles are used without keepers.

Double-jointed and multi-jointed bits

Although double-jointed mouthpieces still apply tongue pressure, they do not have the same squeezing action as their single-jointed counterparts and seem to suit horses with fleshy tongues better, and also many Thoroughbreds. Thoroughbreds who go into training for racing are nearly always ridden in single-jointed snaffles, usually with loose-rings. Some riders who specialise in re-schooling horses off the track say that by substituting a double-jointed snaffle — usually a French link — they set up different pressures on different parts of the mouth, so a horse who has learned to take hold of his racing-snaffle is given something different to think about and react to.

Double-jointed bits do, however, tend to give the rider a less definite 'feel' than those with single joints, which means that some prefer them and others dislike them. One person's definition of a horse who is light in the hand is different from another's, so personal preference has to be taken into account: if you are tempted to take too much rein contact in a French link your horse will resent it, so in this case you might establish better lines of communication with a single-jointed bit.

The main types of double-jointed snaffle are: the French link; those with a half-moon central link; the Dick Christian; snaffles with a central lozenge (notably the KK training bit); the Fillis snaffle; the Dr Bristol. The Dr Bristol stands on its own in that its central link has flat sides designed to give sharper tongue pressure, which is why it is usually classified as a 'strong' snaffle.

While the basically mild French link has a kidney-shaped central plate, those bits with a half-moon jointed mouthpiece are claimed by the importers to be even milder. Although some horses appear to prefer the latter, others seem happy in either.

The Dick Christian is an old design with a small central ring. The traditional mouthing bit is in some respects a Dick Christian with keys on, the keys — designed to encourage a horse to mouth, salivate and accept the bit — being attached to a central ring. The mouthing bit, once used as standard when breaking young horses, is now somewhat out of favour, the main objection from some trainers being that youngsters sometimes play too much with the keys. Although mouthing bits are intended simply to introduce the horse to the *idea* of a bit rather than for riding, some people like to use them for the horse's initial experience under saddle, or as an option to re-educate a horse who sets his jaw against the bit.

The KK training bit, a modern alternative to the traditional mouthing bit, is well made, being designed in a specific attempt to take the layout of the horse's mouth into account and to encourage the horse to mouth and accept the bit without fussing.

The Fillis snaffle, invented by James Fillis, an influential horsemen of the late nineteenth and early twentieth century, deserves greater appreciation. It is suspended in the mouth and has a port (arch) in the centre of the mouthpiece, which is jointed on either side. The port allows room for the tongue but does not, as is sometimes believed, put pressure on the roof of the mouth — and a lot of horses seem to like it.

The Waterford snaffle, sometimes called the 'bobble bit,' is multi-jointed. Although many people think of it as potentially severe, some horses seem to like it and go kindly in it. This may be because, having lots of joints, the mouthpiece is flexible and follows the shape of the horse's mouth, which they find more comfortable.

Roller snaffles

Snaffles with rollers set around or in the mouthpiece are also often described as 'strong' (see *Becoming Strong* in Chapter 9), but most are potentially no more severe than other kinds of mouthpiece. One exception is the Magenis snaffle, which has square-sided arms with rollers set inside each one. On the other hand, the cherry roller snaffle, and snaffles with alternate steel and copper rollers, which are often recommended for strong horses, succeed simply because the horse is unable to lean on the mouthpiece. The constant mobility of the rollers encourages him to salivate and to play with the bit, which in turn often leads to him relaxing his jaw rather than setting it against the rider's hand. However, since jointed roller snaffles have to be made with straight mouthpiece arms, this does give them a definite nutcracker effect.

Mouthpiece Materials

The material from which a mouthpiece is made can have a great influence on its acceptability to the horse.

The herdsmen of Mongolia used bits made from twisted rawhide, with animal horn cheekpieces. The Native Americans also used rawhide, which is strong but becomes soft and slimy when chewed. Perhaps this was an early lesson: if the horse is encouraged to mouth the bit, he will be more comfortable. Archaeologists have found bits made of bronze, dating from around 1500 BC, and also bits of iron. Hardwood has also been used at various times and old horsemen of today can still remember wooden breaking bits with metal keys being used to mouth youngsters for the first time.

Stainless steel

Stainless steel has, for many years, been the most popular material and was initially hailed as the answer to the horseman's prayer because it does not rust or bend. But, although it is hard-wearing and easy to look after, it is not necessarily the best material in all respects: for instance, it is cold and it does not encourage salivation as much as some other materials, such as metals with a copper content.

'Stainless steel is cold to the touch. A lot of horses are more ready to take the bit if you warm it in your hands first' — Gary Singh-Khakhian.

Although you do not necessarily want to see gobbets of foam flying out of a horse's mouth, a certain amount of salivation is necessary if he is to be comfortable. Saliva acts as a lubricant, permitting the bit to slide over the bars of the mouth: if the horse has a very dry mouth, the bit will drag over the skin, causing discomfort and possibly bruising.

Nickel

Nickel bits (actually a mixture of nickel and brass) were the forerunners of today's stainless steel versions. The disadvantages of nickel were that it wore quickly, particularly around the joints, and it could bend.

However, it was warmer than stainless steel and some older horsemen maintain that horses much preferred its taste. In recent years the riding world has woken up to the fact that making a mouthpiece from a material which the horse prefers gives us a headstart in getting him to accept the bit.

Copper and copper alloys

Copper is a favourite for encouraging salivation, but does not wear well. Manufacturers therefore use it either as a coating over stainless steel or to make inserts or rollers; the one disadvantage of the roller snaffle with alternate steel and copper rollers is that the copper rollers wear faster than their neighbours and the bit must be checked regularly to make sure there is no risk of the horse's mouth or tongue being pinched.

It is now possible to buy bits made from alloys with a high copper content. These are usually preferable to bits with copper inserts simply because they are much more hard-wearing. The British company James Cotterell and Sons makes a full range of snaffles in Kangaroo metal, a substantially cupro-nickel alloy, which they claim is as strong and hard-wearing as stainless steel. Certainly, many horses seem to go better in a Kangaroo bit than in a stainless steel version of the same design. This also applies to bits made from 'German silver' and Aurigan by the German company, Sprenger. 'German silver' is 60 per cent copper, while Aurigan is 85 per cent copper. Aurigan is also nickel-free, which means that it can be used for horses who show allergic reactions to nickel — which is uncommon but not unknown. Cyprium bits, the latest arrivals on the market, are 90 per cent copper and are also nickel-free.

One school of thought claims that horses salivate more when ridden in bits with a high copper content because they find the taste unpleasant. However, since so many horses seem more relaxed in their work when ridden in these bits it is hard to give credence to this argument.

Rubber

Rubber snaffles, both jointed and unjointed, are popular with many riders, because they think of them as mild bits. The straight bar rubber snaffle actually bends round the horse's jaw when rein contact is taken up, so one advantage might be that it follows the shape of the horse's mouth. The disadvantage is that some horses tend to lean on it — and neither the straight bar not the jointed variety will stand up to a horse's teeth. Some horses can chew their way through a rubber coating very quickly, even when their teeth do not have sharp edges. Therefore, the straight bar rubber snaffle must have a central metal core so that, if the horse does bite through the rubber, the rider is not left with a bit in two halves.

Jointed rubber snaffles are quite heavy. Some horses seem to like them and are light in the hand, but others become fussy in the mouth or lean on the bit. Again, it all comes down to what makes the individual horse feel comfortable.

Hardened or vulcanised rubber is more hard-wearing than the ordinary, soft kind and makes for a broad, heavy mouthpiece. The half-moon vulcanised snaffle allows more room than the straight bar for the tongue, and a sensitive horse whose mouth is long enough to accommodate the bulky mouthpiece will often go nicely in this bit. As mentioned earlier (*p.24*), swapping between a vulcanised pelham and a vulcanised snaffle works well with some horses.

Nylon and plastics

If you want the broad bearing surface of a fat half-moon snaffle without the weight, a nylon half-moon may provide the answer. These are hard-wearing and much more resistant to horses' teeth than rubber bits.

Plastic mouthpieces have been another big success story of recent years. Materials used by manufacturers such as Nathe and Happy Mouth are pliable but strong, although as always these bits must be checked every time they are used. They are said to encourage salivation and to give the horse confidence to accept a contact – some are even said to be apple flavoured!

Rubber- and plastic-coated bits are now available with a wide choice of cheekpieces, including D-ring, loose-ring and full cheek. One problem to watch out for, which manufacturers either have not spotted or cannot solve, is that loose-rings sometimes jam temporarily. As they are supposed to run freely, this obviously defeats the object of the design.

Cheekpieces

Cheekpiece design is the final part in the equation. The first thing to decide is whether the horse will go better with a bit that stays still in the mouth, or whether he will be happier and less resistant with one which makes constant small movements. Basically, a loose-ring allows more movement while a fixed ring — whether eggbutt, D-ring or full cheek — means that the bit is more stable. Once you have made this decision, you can then decide on a likely combination of mouth-piece and cheekpiece — and hope that your horse follows the same logic. (Choosing bits to suit particular schooling problems is dealt with in Chapter **9.**)

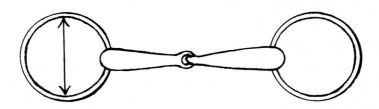

Measuring snaffle rings

Loose-ring designs

Loose-ring cheekpieces can either be wire or flat ring. Wire rings are thinner and move more easily; flat ring snaffles (sometimes known as Irish snaffles) have a slightly more limited movement and are not seen as often as they used to be. Rings range in size from those of bradoons, measuring about 2 1/4 in (55mm), to large ring racing-snaffles, which measure up to 5 in (125mm). The principle behind the racing-snaffle is that the large rings provide extra steering by pressing against the sides of the horse's face.

The steering functions of racing-snaffle rings

The main drawback with loose-ring snaffles is that the horse's lips may be pinched between the ring and the hole. This is more likely to happen with a young or uneducated horse, in whom the steering is still wobbly, or with a rider who relies too heavily on the reins for steering. Rubber bitguards — discs which fit over the rings onto the mouthpiece

— remove the risk. The easiest way to fit them is to soak them in hot water to make the rubber easier to stretch, then slip two thin straps such as spur straps through the centre hole. Use one strap to stretch the disc over the bit ring and the other to provide anchorage.

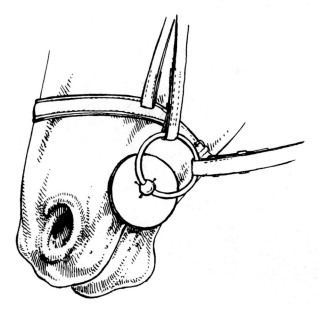

A bitguard in place

Vulcanised half-moon snaffles often have loose-rings, which at first may seem like a contradiction in terms: the mouthpiece is designed to stay still whilst the rings allow movement. In practice, the loose-rings allow just enough movement to prevent the mouthpiece from feeling 'dead' in the horse's mouth.

Wilson and Scorrier snaffles are designed for strong horses. They have two sets of rings — which can be either wire or flat — on each side. The Wilson is primarily a driving bit, while the Scorrier is an adaptation of the design and is occasionally used on riding horses. Also known as the Cornish snaffle, the Scorrier is sometimes made with a serrated mouthpiece. In both bits, the outer rings are no different from those

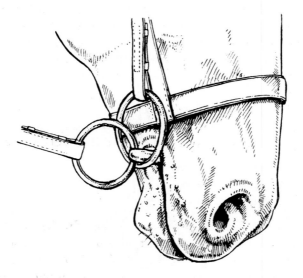

A Wilson snaffle fitted

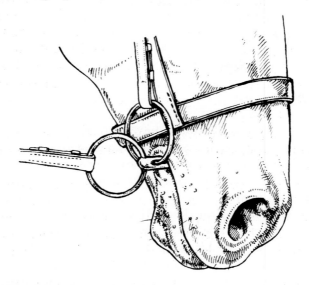

A Scorrier fitted

of an ordinary snaffle. In the Wilson, the inner rings 'float' round the mouthpiece while in the true Scorrier they run through slots set into it. The bridle cheekpieces are usually attached to the inner rings and the reins can be attached either to the outer rings, which gives a potentially severe squeezing action, or to both sets of rings, which lessens the squeezing action.

Four-ring snaffles can have a mild action if used with a Newmarket bridle. Few people will have this item, and it is certainly not on general sale, but saddlery historian Elwyn Hartley Edwards details its use in his book *Saddlery*.

Fixed ring designs

Eggbutt snaffles can have either wire or flat rings. In theory, the wire ring allows a slight degree of movement, but in practice it seems to make little difference. The smooth sides of the eggbutt are designed to eliminate the risk of pinching, though a rough or unbalanced rider can still cause rubbing and bruising. Eggbutt snaffles are a popular choice in riding schools, as novice riders who lack balance and thus have unsteady hands are less likely to cause discomfort to the horse.

Occasionally you may see a slotted eggbutt snaffle, with slots in the top of the rings, through which the bridle cheekpieces are buckled. This arrangement produces poll pressure, rather like a hanging snaffle, and it is surprising that the design is not more readily available — many horses would probably go well in it.

An eggbutt is unlikely to pull through the horse's mouth, unless it is an eggbutt bradoon with small rings. If it is felt there is any risk of this happening, rubber bitguards can be used.

The hanging snaffle, called a Filet Baucher in some catalogues, looks like the top half of a jointed pelham and is designed to produce poll pressure. At the same time, pressure on the tongue is lessened because the bit is suspended in the horse's mouth, which is perhaps why some go well in it. It is available with either single-jointed or French link mouthpieces.

The Fillis snaffle is essentially a form of hanging snaffle. It is comfortable for horses with fat tongues, although they are not the only ones who appreciate the ported, double-jointed mouthpiece. Although the ordinary hanging snaffle is now on the list of permitted bits for dressage tests, sadly the Fillis snaffle is not.

Full cheek snaffles help with steering, especially of young, green or ignorant horses, by putting pressure on the sides of the face. There are three variations: the Fulmer snaffle, the full cheek and the full cheek with eggbutt sides. All are designed to stay still in the horse's mouth, although the Fulmer snaffle — originally known as the Australian loose-ring — offers more play. This is because the rings to which the reins are buckled are loose-rings set outside the mouthpiece. In the Spanish Riding School, the Fulmer snaffle is used in conjunction with a drop noseband because the School believes this is the best fore-runner to the double bridle, which will be used on horses whose schooling has reached an advanced stage.

In theory, all full cheek snaffles should be used with small leather keepers, which attach the tops of the bit cheeks to the bridle cheekpieces and prevent the former from tipping forwards. In practice, they can be used without keepers if you find that the horse goes better that way: without keepers, the bit is less fixed. The danger is that some horses have the habit of grabbing hold of the bottom cheeks if they are allowed to hang free, and this can be dangerous. If the bit gets hooked up on the horse's teeth, he may panic and rear. Should a horse show any incli-nation to do this, fit keepers or use a different bit.

When a full cheek snaffle is used without keepers, the joint hangs lower in the horse's mouth: this is not a good idea if he shows any inclination to try to put his tongue over the bit. When keepers are used, you can adjust the bit a hole lower than it would otherwise need to be, and still ensure that it is at the correct height in the mouth: which can make a surprising difference to the horse's acceptance of this bit.

Modern full cheek snaffles often have a design fault that you will not find in most older snaffles. Originally, the top cheekpiece was angled slightly away at the top edge so that it would not press into the horse's face. However, many modern bits have cheekpieces that are straight up and down, which can cause unwanted pressure if the horse's muzzle is anything but narrow.

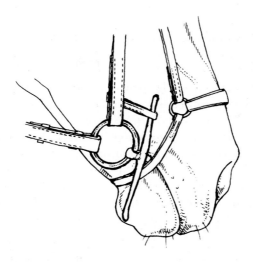

Using keepers with a full cheek snaffle

Spoon cheek and half-spoon cheek snaffles both work in a similar way. Originally designed for trotting horses so that their drivers had more control when racing, they get their names from the shape of the cheeks. Full spoons have cheeks top and bottom to give pressure on the sides of the face, whilst half-spoons are fitted with the cheeks facing downward to give pressure on the outside of the lower jaw. They are available with a variety of mouthpieces, including flexible rubber, single joint and Dr Bristol.

Some horses find the pressure from full cheeks uncomfortable when they are teething, and this outweighs the benefit of better steering. Horses generally may be more comfortable if such bits are used without keepers, if it seems safe to do so — alternatively rubber bitguards can be used. By keeping the bit central and adding gentle pressure to the sides of the lips and muzzle, these guards can help more than many people realise.

The Dexter ring snaffle is essentially a half-spoon cheek snaffle to which a large ring (not unlike that of a Chifney — *see p48*) has been added. The reins are attached to the ordinary bit rings in the normal way. The theory behind the design is that the large ring prevents the horse from catching hold of the bit and choosing his own direction. This bit, which some might consider a 'last resort', is not in general use, but is sometimes employed on hard-pulling, 'one-sided' steeple-chasers.

D-ring snaffles also help with steering, though their action is less definite than that of a full cheek. Because of the angle at which the central joint falls in the mouth, they seem to have a slight lifting action, but they must be adjusted high enough to prevent the horse from getting his tongue over the mouthpiece.

Whether you use a new bit or an old one, check that the cheekpieces or rings run smoothly when they are supposed to, and that there is equal movement on both sides. Occasionally you will find a badly made eggbutt, D-ring or full cheek snaffle, in which one side locks. As this is equivalent to setting one hand on the reins, it must affect the horse's way of going.

GAGS, LEVER SNAFFLES AND LAST RESORTS

Gag Snaffles

The gag snaffle is so different from all the others that it forms a distinct offshoot from the snaffle family of bits. Gag snaffles employ special cheekpieces made from rolled leather or cord, which run through slots at the top and bottom of the rings. These cheekpieces buckle on to the headpiece at one end and fasten to the reins at the other. Looked at logically, this arrangement produces the apparent contradiction of a downward action on the poll and an upward action on the mouthpiece. Despite this, it is a combination which works well in practice for some partnerships.

It is important, however, that gag snaffles are used with two reins; one direct to the bit rings, so that the bit can act in the same way as an ordinary snaffle, and the other to the gag cheeks. Some riders use a single rein to the gag cheeks only, because they say that two reins are too much of a handful cross-country, but by doing this they are putting themselves at risk and making the action of the bit too severe. If a gag cheek breaks — and remember, it has to take more leverage than an ordinary bridle cheekpiece — you are left with no brakes and no steering. As you are likely to be travelling at speed at the time, this is a scenario that does not bear thinking about.

Using two reins also means that you can ride on the direct rein most of the time and employ the gag rein only when you need it. This way, the horse's mouth does not become deadened by a constant upward pull and you can reward him by riding on the direct rein except when necessary.

If it becomes necessary to use the gag rein, think in terms of check and release rather than setting up a constant pull. Giving and taking is far more effective: this applies to any bit, but especially to the gag snaffle.

The most common cheekpieces for gags are eggbutt and loose-ring. Loose-rings give a little more play, but this is limited by the fact that the gag cheekpieces run through their centres. The eggbutt's smooth sides avoid the risk of pinching and are perhaps more logical. Having said that, a lot of event riders use gag snaffles with large loose-rings because they hope that — as with large ring racing-snaffles — these will give extra help with steering.

A loose-ring gag fitted

It is possible to find gag snaffles with full cheeks, but they are rarely seen nowadays. The ultimate must be a double bridle with a gag bradoon, the thought of which would give most riders nightmares. As this could be used only with a single rein to the bradoon and another to the curb, any rider who felt it necessary would have to be in serious trouble.

Gag mouthpieces range from single-jointed, either plain metal or rubber-covered, to those with rollers set round them. Whatever design is used, the rider should not forget that it is possible to pull the bit very high into the horse's mouth, with the potential for a lot of damage.

Polo pony in a gag snaffle

Gag snaffles are a commonly used for polo ponies, often coupled with a drop noseband, plus cavesson noseband and standing martingale.

This arrangement may seem like an overkill to riders in other disciplines, but top players say that they deliberately overbit their ponies so that they are slightly behind the bit and, in their opinion, more manoeuvrable.

Lever Snaffles

There are fashions in bits as in everything else. Every now and then new designs surface, only to disappear again when we discover that they are not the magic wands we hoped for — and we do hope for them, even when we know they cannot possibly exist!

The three-ring snaffle and the American gag are two bits which seem to be here to stay. They are modified forms of the gag snaffle. Both work on the leverage principle and both can exert more or less leverage depending on the rein position used.

The three-ring snaffle has become very popular with show jumpers and eventers, though is not permitted in dressage tests, even on its mildest setting. Also known as the Continental snaffle, Dutch or Belgian gag and even the 'fat lady bit', it is normally used with a single rein. Unlike the classic gag snaffle, this is perfectly safe, because the rein is attached to ordinary bridle cheekpieces rather than sliding ones. The bridle cheekpieces attach to a separate small ring at the top, rather like that on a pelham, so some poll pressure is applied automatically.

The top ring of the bit is the largest one, and when the rein is attached to it this gives less leverage than when the rein is attached to either of the lower rings. Occasionally, you may see this bit used with two reins rather like a pelham or double bridle, with the 'bradoon' rein on the top ring and the 'curb' rein on the bottom ring. Another variation is to use pelham roundings (leather couplings) on the top and bottom rings, with a single rein.

'I've used this bit successfully on horses who try to lean on the rider's hands. By starting off a schooling session with the reins on one of the two lower rings, you can get the horse working correctly and then reward him by switching the reins to the top ring' — Kate Moore, event rider and show producer.

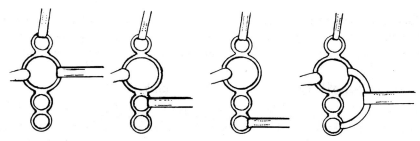

Options for rein attachments to a three-ring gag

The American gag works on a similar principle to the three-ring, but has sliding rather than fixed cheeks, giving more movement. This bit has two rein positions although, again, it can be used with double reins, or with pelham roundings to each ring and a single rein.

Both the three-ring and the American gag are available with a huge variety of jointed and unjointed mouthpieces, including single-jointed, French link, rubber-covered, Happy Mouth and Nathe.

Last Resorts

There are a few bits which come under the general heading of the snaffle, but which could never be described as mild, even in the most skilled hands. The twisted snaffle, once commonplace but now rarely seen, is one of them; *perhaps* a skilled rider can use one without inflicting damage, but such skill is rare and the twisted snaffle should come into the category of 'not for general use'.

The chain-mouth snaffle is even worse, and deserves mention only to draw attention to the lengths to which some bit manufacturers — and presumably riders — are prepared to go. It consists of two bit rings joined by a chain similar to a curb chain.

The W-mouth snaffle is another last resort that most riders will never see, let alone use. It consists of a pair of loose-rings with two single-jointed mouthpieces; each mouthpiece having one short and one long arm. These arms are matched to their opposites so that when the rider takes a contact the result is a W-shape, with a joint on each side of the tongue and arms pressing on the bars.

BITTING YOUNGSTERS

In an ideal world, young horses would be taught to lead correctly almost from the day they were born. If they miss out on basic education, you face all sorts of problems trying to teach a big, stroppy yearling (or an older horse, for that matter) that he cannot drag you around as if you were simply an inconvenience at the end of a lead rope. Once they are faced with such problems, many people resort to a Chifney, a bit traditionally used on colts and stallions to prevent them from rearing whilst being led. This bit has a large ring mouthpiece which surrounds the lower jaw, the lead rein being fastened to a smaller ring at its base. The Chifney should only be used for leading, never for riding, and it must be employed with great care, since it has the potential to do immense damage in rough hands.

Even if a youngster is educated correctly, there may well be occasions when a headcollar— even one of the special controller headcollars which put pressure on nose and poll until the horse stops pulling — is not enough. Any horse can become excited or full of his own importance, so it is sensible to introduce a bit before the horse is three years old and ready to be backed.

When to Start

Some people like to bit a yearling, while others prefer to leave it until the horse is two. If you want to show the horse in hand, he will need to be accustomed to wearing a bridle and being led in it. Two-year-olds wear bridles as a matter of course in the show ring and this is also generally considered more acceptable for yearlings, although a leather headcollar may be used if you have a particular reason — and can be sure of having enough control!

Before introducing a bit, have the horse's mouth and teeth checked by a good equine vet or equine dentist. Any sharp edges can be floated (rasped) and other problems can be spotted and dealt with. If a horse's first experiences of wearing a bit are associated with pain or discomfort, you are establishing memories that will take a long time to fade, and which may never be fully erased.

Which Bit To Use

There are no hard and fast rules about the type of bit you start off with, apart from the fact that it should be some form of plain snaffle. The common choices are either a traditional breaking bit with keys on the mouthpiece, some form of half-moon snaffle or a single-jointed snaffle. Although using a breaking bit for the first few times seems to work well with most horses, all trainers have their likes and dislikes. If you are working under the guidance of someone who prefers to use an ordinary bit right from the beginning, and whose methods are proven with a variety of young horses, then follow this example.

The breaking bit is designed mainly to encourage the horse to play with the mouthpiece and accept it. If you do not want to use it, or are ready to move on to the next stage, a half-moon bit is often a good choice, particularly if the horse is being led rather than ridden. This stays high enough in the mouth to dissuade the horse from putting his tongue over it. A lightweight mouthpiece, such as a nylon, Nathe or Happy Mouth, is comfortable for most youngsters.

Introducing a Bit

There are several ways of getting the horse to wear a bit without startling or frightening him, but all require a handler who will stay calm and move quietly. Anyone who expects trouble is likely to meet

49

it, so think positively and avoid making hesitant or jerky movements.

You can either use a bridle from day one, or, if for some reason you do not want to, you can start off with a headcollar fitted with straps or clips to hold the bit. There is generally no reason not to use a bridle, but keep the process of fitting it simple and take things one step at a time. Make sure that the browband is going to be long enough to avoid pinching the horse's ears, and remove the noseband altogether. Before attempting to add a bit, get the horse used to this 'half-bridle' going over his head, and to his ears being placed gently between browband and headpiece. Remove the bridle with as much care, and repeat the process until the horse accepts it as nothing out of the ordinary. Holding the bridle alongside the horse's head will then give you a rough idea of any adjustments that need to be made before the bit is fitted.

It makes sense to try to make wearing a bit as pleasant an experience for the horse as possible (or at least to minimise his objections!) Time-honoured ways include dipping a bit in warm water and then in sugar or salt, or coating it in molasses or treacle.

Horses naturally investigate things with their lips, and many will take the bit without persuasion. If a horse is calm but unco-operative, tickling his tongue through the side of his mouth is often a more effective way of persuading him to open his mouth than the traditional method of pressing down on the bars.

Occasionally a horse will be suspicious or reluctant, and will raise his head out of reach. In this case, put on the 'half-bridle' to which he is already accustomed, then buckle the bit to one cheekpiece. Standing on the other side, and making sure that the bit cannot bang him on the nose, ask him to open his mouth as before. When he does, gently slip the bit in and fasten it to the other cheekpiece.

Whatever method you use for introducing the bit, be equally careful about removing the bridle. If the bit gets caught on the horse's teeth, he will be frightened. With a horse who was suspicious or nervous to start with, it is sometimes best to undo one cheekpiece and let the bit slip out of his mouth before removing the bridle. Again, be careful not to let the bit bang against his face.

As ever, it is important that the bit fits correctly. When asking a horse to wear one for the first time, the most important thing is to make sure it will not pinch him: if you are not sure whether he will take a five or a five-and-a-half inch (**125** or **140**mm), use the latter.If this proves to be too big, you can soon exchange it for a smaller one, but if you start off by pinching the horse he will have every reason for not wanting to repeat the experience.

Remember that horses' mouths grow along with the rest of them. The yearling who takes a five inch mouthpiece may well need a larger one as he gets bigger.

All horses should be accustomed to being handled, led, tacked up and so on from both sides, so that you can use whichever is safer in a particular set of circumstances. Furthermore, it is essential to ensure that a young horse does not become one-sided through being led only from one side only (usually, the nearside). To prevent this, once the horse has accepted the bit, use a coupling to link the bit rings behind the jaw and fasten the lead rein to this, rather than direct to the bit ring.

THE INFLUENCE OF NOSEBANDS

Nosebands can have a significant effect on the way in which a snaffle acts. Some types can, for example, help to keep the bit central in the horse's mouth and/or prevent him from opening his mouth too wide. It follows, therefore, that the noseband should be chosen with reference to the bit, and fitted with just as much care.

'Someone turned up to a lesson with a rope noseband on her horse. When I asked her why, she said she thought it looked different and made the horse stand out from the crowd!' — international show jumping trainer who prefers to remain nameless...

The most common types of noseband are the cavesson, the drop, the Flash and the Grakle.One of these should suit most combinations. Other, less frequently seen designs such as the Kineton (or Puckle) and the Australian cheeker can also helpto solve specific problems.

Uses and Abuses

At one time most horses were ridden in cavesson nosebands, the simplest design of all. Now you are much more likely to see a snaffle combined with a noseband that has some sort of drop action; in particular, many riders will fit a Flash noseband as their first choice without considering whether or not the horse needs it. The ironic thing is that some horses go far better in a cavesson and resent any noseband which fastens below the bit — especially if, as so often happens, it is fastened too tightly.

To go right back to the beginning, we all want our horses to accept the bit. In order to do so, the horse has to work from behind into the rein, and to relax his jaw. Relaxing the jaw means he needs to mouth the bit, which in turn means he needs a certain amount of freedom. Yet how many horses do you see with their mouths strapped shut so tightly that they continually fight the restraining strap? If this were loosened, or removed, they might well stop fighting and accept the bit far more readily. In this scenario, the noseband creates the very problem it is designed to prevent.

Obviously, you cannot have a horse opening his mouth wide and yawing at the bit, but his mouth should not be permanently shut tight. If he has learned to open his mouth too wide to evade the bit, then a noseband which prevents that may be necessary but, as a first step, try a broad, flat cavesson noseband adjusted a hole lower and a hole tighter than usual. You should still be able to slide a finger between the noseband and the horse's face. This sometimes works better than a noseband with a drop strap, because although it puts pressure on the nose and jaw when necessary, the horse does not resent it. Another alternative is a doubleback or cinch cavesson, which doubles back on itself behind the jaw and is easy to adjust so that it is snug but not uncomfortable.

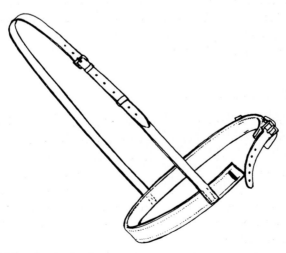

The doubleback or cinch cavesson

If this does not work, one of the drop nosebands may do the trick so long as it is fitted correctly. It must not interfere with the bit rings — a particular problem with drop nosebands if the proportions are not exactly right for that particular horse. Neither should it rub the cheekbones nor interfere with the horse's breathing.

Common Nosebands and Their Actions

Broadly speaking, the Flash, drop and Grakle are all designed to give the rider extra control but, since they do it through different control points, you need to choose the one which addresses your horse's particular evasion.

The Flash

The Flash noseband has the vaguest action, which may be why some horses resent it less than the others. One of its virtues is that it helps to keep the bit central in the horse's mouth, which is why it is popular with many dressage riders who use loose-ring snaffles and are not allowed to fit bitguards in competition. However, the Flash only works correctly if the cavesson part is sufficiently substantial: too many are narrow and flimsy so, as soon as the drop strap is fastened, the cavesson is pulled down the horse's nose.

The drop

The drop noseband is favoured by the Spanish Riding School. When used with a Fulmer or full cheek snaffle it solves the problem of bit cheeks getting trapped under a cavesson noseband, or the cavesson part of a Flash. If the strap across the front of the nose is too wide, it may interfere with the bit rings so, if a standard size does not fit, ask a saddler to make one that is adjustable across the front as well as the back.

The Grakle

Grakle or crossover nosebands come in two styles. The more common

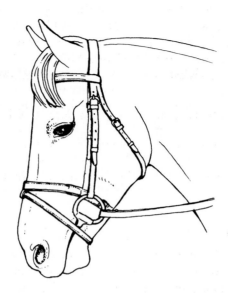

*The Flash
noseband*

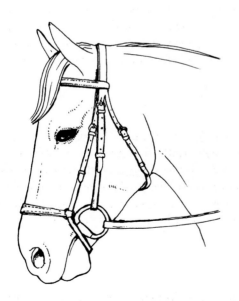

*The drop
noseband*

fits under the cheekbones at the top and crosses midway down the centre of the face, while the other type – sometimes called the American Grakle – fits higher at the top. Many event riders who opt for a Grakle to give more control cross-country are choosing the American Grakle because they find the horse accepts it more readily. One reason for this may be that standard Grakles are often fitted a hole too high at the top, so that the upper straps rub the horse's facial bones. The advantage of a Grakle is that it does not interfere with the bit rings or cheekpieces, so a Fulmer or full cheek snaffle will not be trapped underneath it. At present, it is only allowed for dressage tests under horse trials rules, whereas the Flash, drop (and, of course, cavesson) nosebands are permitted for all tests where a snaffle is mandatory or optional.

The Grakle noseband

These nosebands are all in general use in combination with snaffle bits. Ideally, the drop, Flash and Grakle should only be used with snaffles, because the drop straps interfere with the curb action of a pelham or kimblewick, and would be drastic overkill with a double bridle. In recent years it has become more acceptable to use a Flash or Grakle with a pelham, especially in eventing and show jumping circles. As always, the argument that 'top riders do it' perhaps applies only if your riding skills match up to theirs

Other Types of Noseband and Control

There are several other interesting nosebands which, in the right hands, can make the difference between being in or out of control.

The Kineton

The Kineton, or Puckle, comes under the 'Help, no brakes' category and should only be used by experienced and competent riders who appreciate its potential severity. The Kineton is unusual in that it does not rely on keeping the horse's mouth closed to give greater control, and in this respect it can sometimes work on a horse who pulls hard in situations such as cross-country but resents any form of noseband which fastens below the bit. It consists of two U-shaped metal loops connected by a strap which goes across the horse's nose and is adjusted so that the loops are in contact with the bit rings but do not pull them up. This usually means that the front strap is at roughly the same height as a correctly adjusted drop noseband; about 3in (8cm) above the top of the nostrils and high enough not to interfere with the horse's breathing.

When the rider takes a rein contact, pressure is transferred to the noseband. The harder the horse pulls, or the higher he puts his head in the air, the greater the pressure. When he lowers his head or gives to the rein and is rewarded by the rider giving to him, the pressure is relieved.

It used to be said that the Kineton should only be used with a straight bar or mullen mouth snaffle made from a rigid material, such as metal or stainless steel, but it is often seen in conjunction with jointed snaffles. An unjointed mouthpiece must be a kinder choice, since it limits the amount of pressure that can be put on the nose. The Kineton must be used with care, as the metal loops can cause bruising in rough hands.

The Kineton noseband

The Newmarket bridle

According to saddlery historian Elwyn Hartley Edwards, the Newmarket bridle was used with a four-ring snaffle to persuade the horse to adopt a lower head carriage — but in this situation, the snaffle has a mild action. To obtain this effect the reins are attached to the ordinary snaffle rings whilst the inner, loose pair are connected by an adjustable noseband strap. Some of the pressure is thus taken on the nose which is, after all, the control point to which a young horse is first accustomed. If the reins are attached to the loose-rings rather than the ordinary ones, the nose becomes the main control point and there is minimum pressure on the mouth.

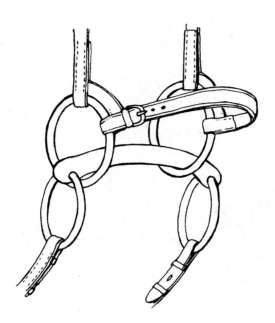

The Newmarket bridle

The Australian cheeker

The Australian cheeker is used in conjunction with a snaffle on hard-pulling horses. It is seen mainly on the racetrack, but has also filtered through to the worlds of show jumping and eventing. No one could call it severe, because it consists simply of two rubber bitguards joined by a central strap, which runs down the centre of the horse's face and fastens to the bridle headpiece. The theory behind the Australian cheeker is that the horse can see the central strap and backs off it, so the effect of the noseband is mainly psychological. However, it also ensures that the bit cannot drop too low in the horse's mouth, so it is sometimes used on animals who try to put their tongues over the bit.

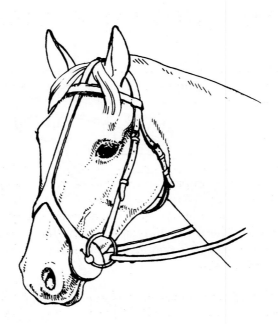

The Australian cheeker

AUXILIARY AIDS AND BIT ACTION

As with nosebands, martingales and training equipment have a significant influence on bit action — a fact not always fully appreciated by those who use them.

Martingales

Martingales have become accepted as a standard piece of tack in many spheres, especially show jumping and cross-country – although they are not permitted for dressage. Most riders use them without really thinking about the effect they have on the bit and the rider's rein aids, which can be considerable. There is nothing wrong with using a correctly fitted martingale, and sometimes it may be essential, but it can be an eye-opener to ride without one.

Photographs taken fifty years ago show riders using snaffle bridles with cavesson nosebands, with two pairs of reins on the snaffle rings, the lower pair passing through the rings of a running martingale. The reins are held in the same way as for a double bridle, with the martingale rein as the lower or 'curb' one. The idea was that the rider had an independent rein as well as one affected by the martingale, but this practice has virtually died out.

The standing martingale attaches to the girth and to a cavesson noseband, or to the cavesson part of a Flash — never to a drop noseband or the bottom part of a Flash, where it would restrict the horse's breathing when it came into play. It acts on the nose but has no direct action on the bit, which is why some trainers champion its cause. A snaffle and standing martingale can give the rider extra control when riding a young or difficult horse who tries to throw up his head.

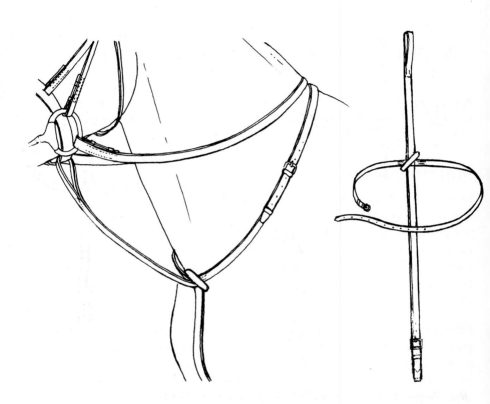

Standing martingale

Rubber rein stops should be used with running and bib martingales to prevent the rings from sliding too far down the reins and interfering with the snaffle rings or cheeks. If you use a Fulmer or full cheek snaffle without keepers, there is a very small but horrifying risk that the martingale rings could get caught on the end of the bit cheeks — so rein stops are essential.

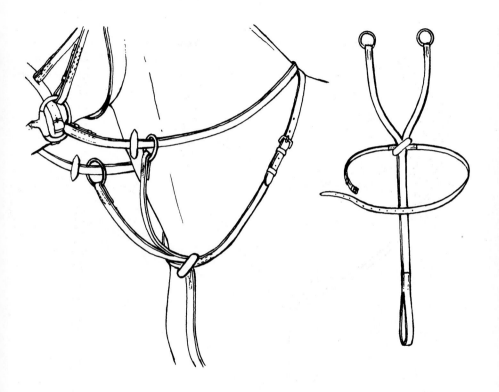

Running martingale, showing rings and rein stops

The combination of a snaffle and martingale need not be severe. In fact, in some circumstances, it can even be kinder than riding in a plain snaffle. A running martingale can act as a buffer between the horse's mouth and the unsteady hands of a novice (or unskilled) rider who does not have an independent seat and uses his or her hands as a balancing aid. When used with an eggbutt snaffle, which stays relatively still in the mouth and has smooth sides, it minimises the damage.

63

The Market Harborough

The Market Harborough is often dismissed or criticised as severe, which is unfair — it can be very effective on a horse who tries to put his head in the air and tank off, but so long as it is adjusted correctly there is no severity. The beauty of it is that it is operated by the horse rather than the rider, so unlike draw or running reins it cannot be used

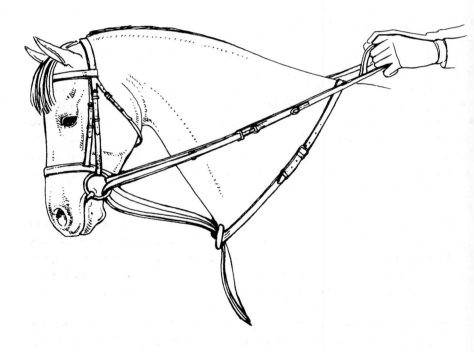

The Market Harborough

inadvertently. It starts from the girth, like a martingale, then divides into two straps, each with a clip at the end. These straps pass through the bit rings and clip on to small D-rings stitched to the reins. When the horse raises his head to pull or resist, the Market Harborough puts pressure on the bars of the mouth via the snaffle. As soon as he lowers his head and relaxes his jaw, the Market Harborough no longer acts.

The Market Harborough should only be used with an ordinary snaffle, not a gag snaffle (see next chapter on braking problems), or any bit with a curb action. Anything other than a plain snaffle would be potentially too severe and could lead to resistances such as overbending (see *Behind The Bit* in Chapter 9).

Bitting and Training Aids

Training aids — or gadgets, depending on your philosophy — can be a minefield. Some trainers condemn them; a few profess to condemn them because they think they should, but use them all the same; others keep an open mind. In an ideal world, all horses would be schooled to go perfectly in a plain snaffle with no 'extras'. In the real world, it does not always work out that way, so there is a lot to be said for keeping an open mind. While this is not the place to discuss training aids in detail, here are some thoughts on their relationships with snaffle bits.

● Training aids should always be used with simple snaffles, and only by riders with independent seats who understand what they are trying to achieve. Whether riding or lungeing, it is more important than ever that the horse is kept moving forwards — otherwise, he will end up tucking his nose in and going nowhere.

● Long-reining a horse in a snaffle is an excellent way of teaching him to accept the bit and to start, stop and steer without the added complication of the rider's weight.

● If a horse is reluctant to take a contact, working him on the lunge in side reins and a snaffle which stays still in the mouth — such as an eggbutt, full cheek or mullen mouth — may give him the confidence he needs.

- If lungeing from the bit, the only type to use is some sort of plain snaffle. The lunge rein puts too much pressure on a lever snaffle or bit with a curb action, because the trainer is so far away from the horse.

- If the lunge rein is fitted through the inside bit ring, over the poll and fastened to the outside bit ring, this gives a modified form of a gag snaffle's action and is potentially quite severe.

- If draw reins are fitted so they go over the poll, down the cheeks, through the bit rings and back to the rider's hands, this will put pressure on the poll and leverage on the bit, so that it acts in a similar way to a gag snaffle.

- Draw and running reins are usually fitted so that they run from the inside of the bit rings to the outside. If they run from outside to inside, they have a more severe squeezing action on the mouth.

- Whatever fitting you choose, always use draw and running reins in conjunction with an ordinary, direct rein to the snaffle ring. Hold the two reins like those of a double bridle, with the direct rein on top, so that it is the dominant one.

- Any snaffle used in conjunction with draw and running reins must have large enough rings to accommodate two pairs of reins — which makes a Fulmer or full cheek design impractical, as the reins can lock. If you want the steering power full cheeks give, try a D-ring snaffle, or use rubber bitguards in conjunction with a loose-ring or eggbutt.

PROBLEM-SOLVING WITH SNAFFLES

The type of snaffle you choose can play an important part in encouraging your horse to accept the bit and work happily and comfortably. It can also help to solve a schooling problem — although, unfortunately, there is no such thing as an instant fix. Changing from one snaffle to another will not cause your horse to suddenly come on to the bit, or stop resisting, but it might well be one of the factors that helps you to put the whole picture together.

Preliminary Checks

If you are having schooling problems, first rule out the obvious causes. These include:

● Physical problems. If the horse is suffering discomfort or even pain, he will find it hard to work correctly.

● Badly fitting tack. This covers anything from too tight a browband, that pinches the ears, to a damaged or badly fitting saddle.

● Over-exuberance caused by too much food, often coupled with too little work.

● Lack of understanding. You may know what you want the horse to do, but does he understand what you are asking him?

● Tiredness and/or boredom. Are you so keen to progress in your schooling that you have locked into the 'trotting round in circles' syndrome?

● Poor riding. We always blame ourselves last, but we all make mistakes and fall into bad habits. Everyone needs a good teacher, or at least someone experienced who can act as 'eyes on the ground'.

Problems and Suggestions

If you decide that a change of tack might help, the following suggestions for dealing with common problems may be useful. Since horses are individuals, some experimentation may be necessary, but do not get into the habit of chopping and changing tack for the sake of it, and look for improvement, rather than 'miracle cures'.

Above the bit

Some horses are above the bit most of the time, while others resist only momentarily — usually when you ask for a transition. In both cases, a snaffle which gives constant slight movement in the mouth is a better choice than one which remains still, as it is more difficult for the horse to set himself above it.

Good choices include a loose-ring single-jointed or French link snaffle. If the horse opens his mouth too wide to try to evade the bit, you may want to use a Flash or drop noseband for a while — but do not assume that this has to be a permanent fixture.

The horse who comes above the bit is often tense through the back and not working through from behind. Incorporate lots of transitions into your schooling and hacking: if he comes above the bit when you ask for a transition, it may help initially if you ask him to come a little deeper in front before making the change up or down.

Some trainers like to use three-ring snaffles, feeling that poll pressure helps to keep the horse in a rounded outline. The danger is that if he is not ridden forwards enough, he will tuck in his nose but still be above the bit.

Lungeing in a loose-ring snaffle and a chambon often helps to persuade this sort of horse to stretch his topline.

Behind the bit

The horse who tucks in his nose and comes behind the bit is not accepting a contact. This may be because he is uncomfortable in his mouth, or it may be that he has been winched in with draw reins or other training aids. Some horses soon work out that they can evade side reins on the lunge by coming behind the bit, often because they are not being worked correctly.

Switching to a bit that remains still in the mouth may give him more confidence but, as always, he must be ridden forwards. Options include eggbutt, Fulmer and full cheek jointed snaffles, or snaffles with mullen mouthpieces. Nathe and Happy Mouth mullen mouth snaffles often work well.

You also have to take into account your own reactions. While many horses are happy in French link snaffles, some riders cannot adjust to the less definite feel they give, and take too strong a contact to try to make this more definite. In such cases, horse and rider may both be more comfortable with a single-jointed or mullen mouth snaffle.

Bolting

The horse who is a true bolter is a very different proposition from one who is simply strong (see separate reference). A horse who bolts is in a blind panic, and the choice of tack will probably make little difference. However, there are stories of bolters who have been cured by fitting an Australian cheeker.

Bolters are dangerous, to themselves and to their riders. The only people who should attempt to re-school them are specialists who appreciate that the problem is first and foremost a mental one. A horse who bolts is not being naughty; he is obeying his natural instinct of fleeing from something that frightens him.

Crossing or setting the jaw

This is often a reaction to discomfort, too much mental pressure, or a rider who tries to force the horse into an outline with the reins. When obvious causes have been eliminated, go back to basics and include plenty of transitions in your work, being extra careful to concentrate on riding forwards into a light rein contact. Trotting poles and small jumping grids can sometimes help to get the horse using his back end — and, at the same time, to take the rider's mind off fiddling with the reins!

A loose-ring snaffle will often be more effective than a fixed one. With a horse who crosses his jaw and pulls, you may want to use a Grakle noseband — especially in situations where you think you may lose control, such as jumping cross-country. If you are not committed to using a snaffle, you may find some horses less resistant in a pelham, preferably used with two reins.

Leaning on the bit

The horse who leans on the bit is inevitably on his forehand, so the immediate aim must be to get him working from behind, which will make him lighter in front. Once again, plenty of transitions and half-halts are the secret. If the horse is physically mature enough to take the work, trotting poles with alternate ends raised 6–12in (15–30cm) will help encourage him to work from behind, but this is hard work for a young horse and should be done in moderation.

A young horse who has just started his education is highly likely to be on his forehand to begin with, as he has to learn to adjust to the rider's weight. Conformation can also play a part: the horse who is croup-high ('built downhill') is at a disadvantage to start with. With such horses, it is necessary to take a realistic view. There is no bit on earth which can alter the skeletal structure of the horse. Remember, however, that horses grow in fits and starts, and a youngster who is 'bum-high' may, quite literally, 'grow out of it'.

Whatever the reason for the horse leaning on the bit, avoid any type of snaffle that stays still in the mouth, since he will find this easier to lean on. Instead, use a loose-ring snaffle with a single or double joint, or one with rollers set around the mouthpiece.

Some trainers recommend using draw reins, fitted so that they run through the bit rings, over the poll and back to the rider's hands. If these are fitted, they should be used in conjunction with a direct rein to the bit.

Rearing

This is an 'experts only' problem — and one which many experts will not want to take on. British problem horse expert Richard Maxwell is one of the few people who has lasting success in curing horses who rear for psychological and physical reasons.

Generally, horses rear for a reason. The aim of anyone attempting to cure them is to discover the cause and remove it. Therefore, if a horse starts rearing, it is vital to check the fit of his tack and to have him examined thoroughly by your vet to rule out any physical causes.

With these steps behind you, make sure that the rider is not using so much hand that the only resistance open to the horse is to go up. Fit a mild snaffle and a standing martingale and only use a rider who can be guaranteed to ride the horse forwards into a light hand and to retain balance if the horse does go up.

Becoming strong

A lot of riders say that their horses are strong when, in fact, they are on the forehand — in which case the tactics outlined in Leaning on the Bit will help.

There are also many riders who make their horses strong by relying too much on the reins. It may be hard to accept that you still need to ride a strong or onward-bound horse forwards from the leg — but it is the only way to establish communication. If he becomes strong in a schooling situation, perhaps in canter, circle work with plenty of transitions from trot to canter and *forwards* to trot again will help.

Trying to ride a decorous half-halt on a horse who is tanking across a field may seem unrealistic, but the principles are still the same: try not to use more hand than leg, and give and take rather than set up a continuous pull. The race rider's technique of bridging the reins helps, particularly if you are a small rider on a big horse: it gives a secure base without pulling and means that the horse pulls against himself rather than against you.

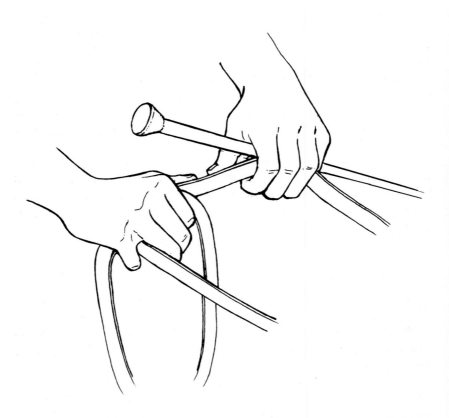

Bridging the reins

Choose your combination of snaffle and noseband according to the horse's way of resisting. For example, a roller snaffle can be effective with a horse who leans as he pulls. Many event riders and show jumpers like to use a three-ring snaffle because the poll pressure and leverage give extra control. Grakle and Kineton nosebands can be useful in some cases, whilst the Australian cheeker is mild but can be particularly effective. The KK correction bit is designed to give more control over strong horses without exerting leverage.

With the horse who tries to put his head in the air and tow you into a fence, a period in a plain snaffle and Market Harborough may help. Another factor which can make a horse strong in front of a fence is 'booting' with spurs on every approach, rather than giving correct, supportive leg aids. Some cross-country trainers say that many of their pupils do this initially 'in case he tries to stop' but a horse is far more likely to jump safely and correctly if he is ridden between leg and hand rather than being provoked into charging the fence in a hollow outline.

Finally, if you continue to find a horse a strong ride, you have to ask yourself whether you are overhorsed. Top professionals can and do ride horses of all shapes and sizes, but there are times when a small rider and a big, powerful horse just do not make a sensible combination.

Tongue evasions

Putting the tongue over the bit, drawing it back under the mouthpiece or hanging it out of the side of the mouth are habits which stem originally from discomfort. It may be that the horse had or has ulcers or sharp teeth, or that he has worn or is wearing a bit that is too big and/or fitted too low.

Whatever the underlying reason for these habits, once they are established they can be difficult — or impossible — to break. Therefore, corrective steps should be taken as soon as the evasion is first noticed. Apart from physical checks of the mouth, the first thing to do is check that the snaffle is the right size, and then that it is adjusted high enough (see *Fitting A Snaffle* in Chapter 2). The type of bit used can also make a big difference; for instance, a mullen mouthpiece will naturally rest higher in the centre than a single-jointed one, and may solve the problem.

If you have a particular reason for using a single-jointed snaffle, it may be worth trying a full cheek or Fulmer snaffle with keepers. The keepers ensure that the joint remains higher in the mouth than it would be if the bit cheeks were free. An Australian cheeker noseband also prevents the bit from dropping too low.

Some horses resent tongue pressure and are happiest in a bit which minimises this. Options include a French link snaffle, a hanging snaffle or a Fillis snaffle. Other horses respond to a roller mouthpiece; either alternate copper and steel rollers or a cherry roller.

Tongue ports (or layers) and tongue grids work with some horses, but others resent them. The simplest form is a rubber tongue port which fastens to the centre of the mouthpiece and lays the tongue flat. That, at any rate, is the theory, but some horses learn to push it to one side and carry on regardless. Metal tongue grids require a separate bridle sliphead; neither they nor tongue ports are permitted for dressage.

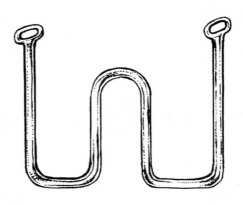

A tongue grid

BIT-BY-BIT GUIDE

Bradoons

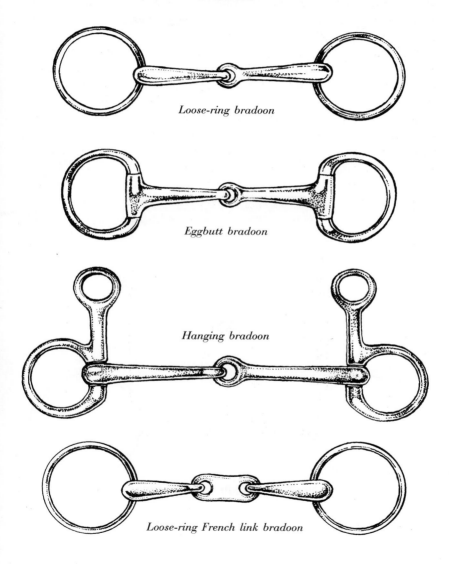

Loose-ring bradoon

Eggbutt bradoon

Hanging bradoon

Loose-ring French link bradoon

Straight bar flexible rubber loose-ring

Straight bar vulcanite loose-ring

Straight bar Happy Mouth loose-ring

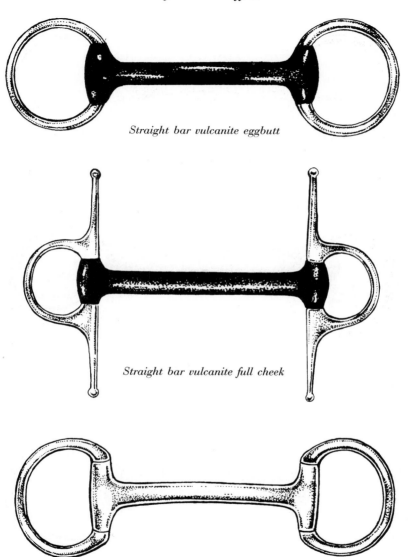

Straight bar vulcanite eggbutt

Straight bar vulcanite full cheek

Mullen mouth stainless steel eggbutt

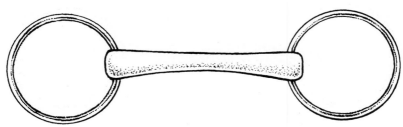

Mullen mouth Nathe loose-ring

Flexible rubber half-spoon

KK snaffle with port

Single-jointed Snaffles

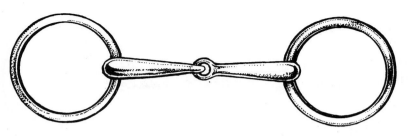

Medium mouth flat loose-ring

Hollow mouth loose wire ring

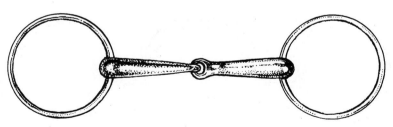

Copper-coated loose-ring

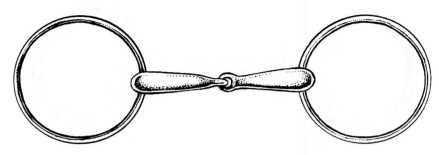

Racing-snaffle with large loose-rings

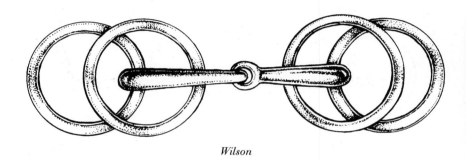

Wilson

Scorrier

Single-jointed Snaffles

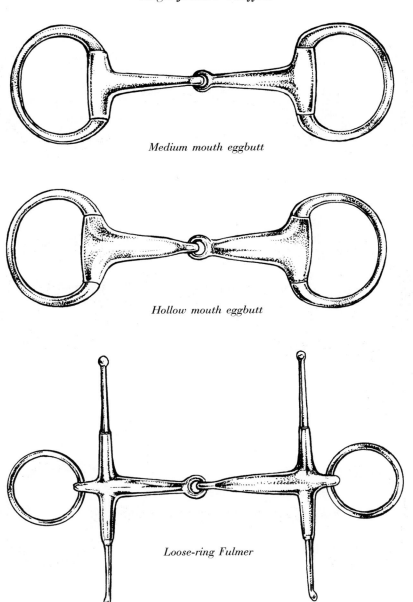

Medium mouth eggbutt

Hollow mouth eggbutt

Loose-ring Fulmer

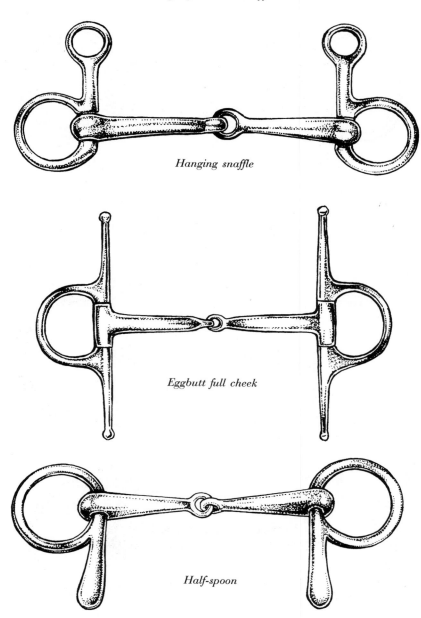

Hanging snaffle

Eggbutt full cheek

Half-spoon

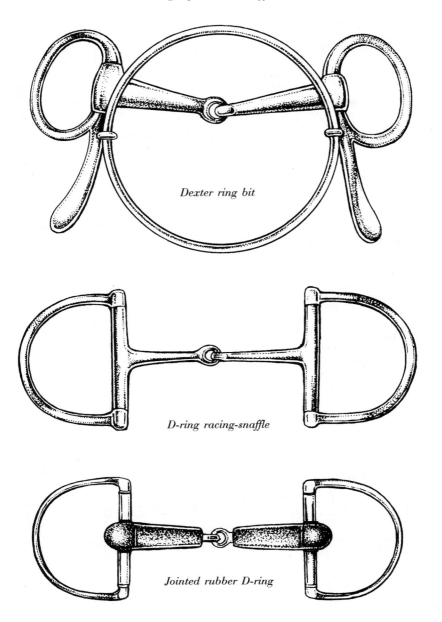

Dexter ring bit

D-ring racing-snaffle

Jointed rubber D-ring

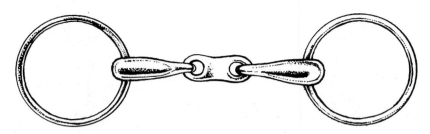

French link loose-ring

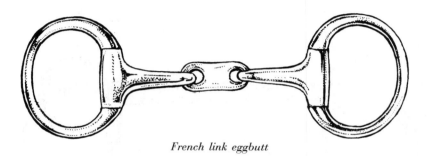

French link eggbutt

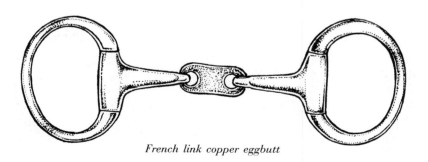

French link copper eggbutt

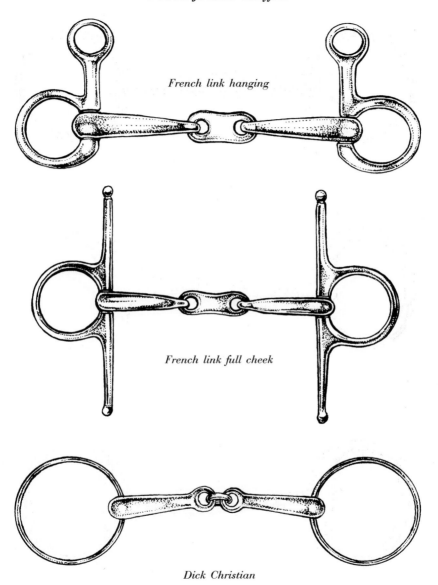

French link hanging

French link full cheek

Dick Christian

KK schooling bit

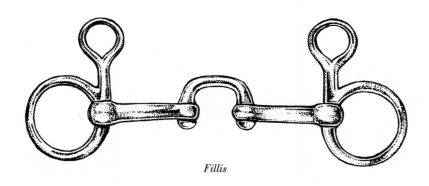

Fillis

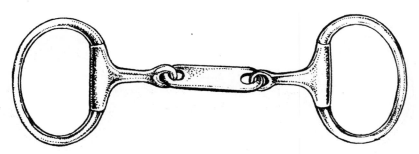

Dr Bristol eggbutt

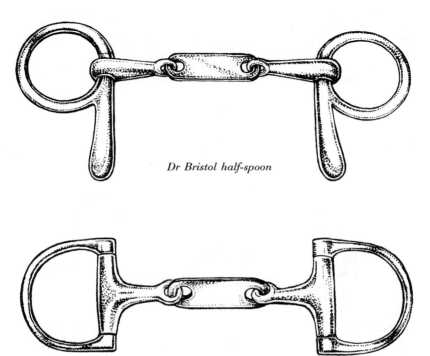

Dr Bristol half-spoon

Dr Bristol D-ring

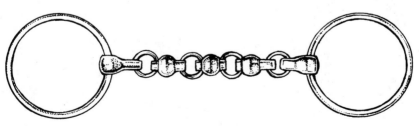

Waterford

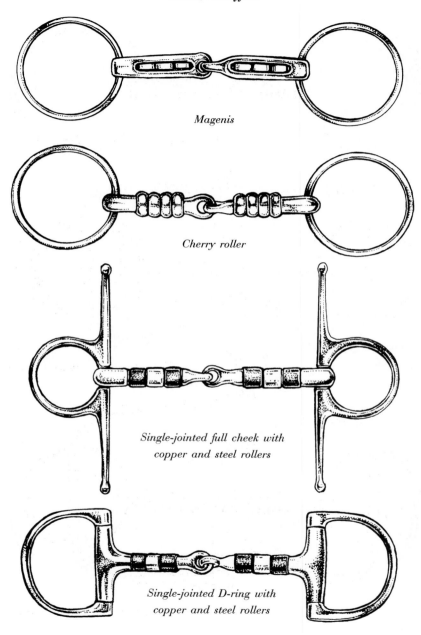

Magenis

Cherry roller

Single-jointed full cheek with copper and steel rollers

Single-jointed D-ring with copper and steel rollers

Gag Snaffles

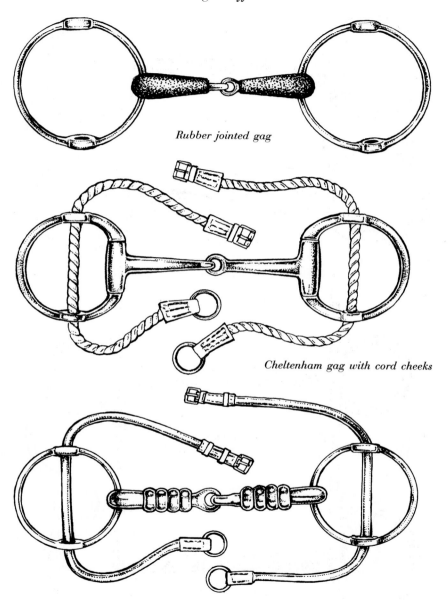

Rubber jointed gag

Cheltenham gag with cord cheeks

Cherry roller gag with rolled leather cheeks

Gag Snaffles

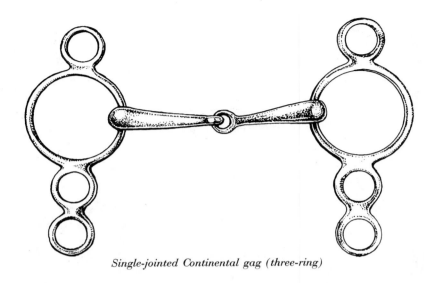

Single-jointed Continental gag (three-ring)

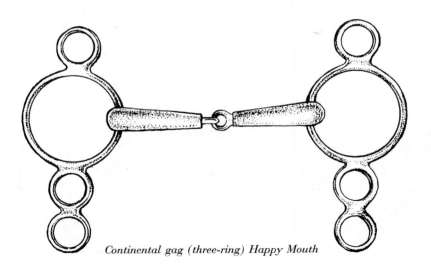

Continental gag (three-ring) Happy Mouth

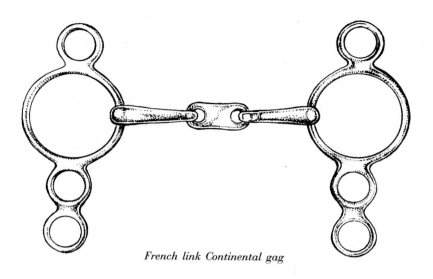

French link Continental gag

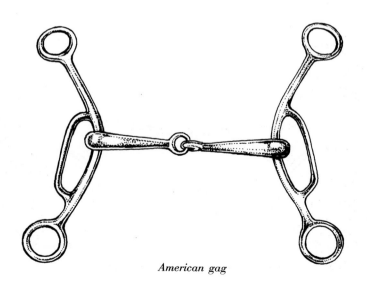

American gag

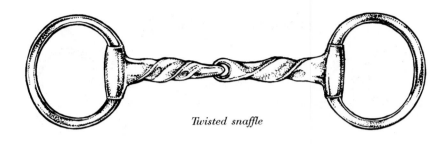

Twisted snaffle

Chain snaffle

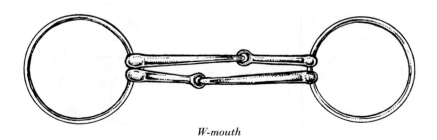

W-mouth

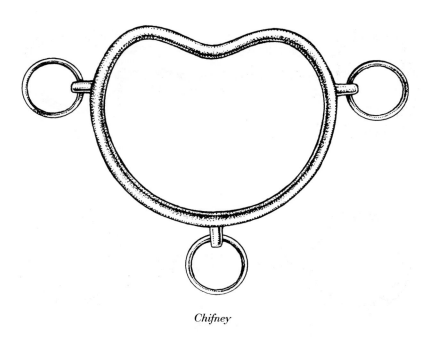

Chifney

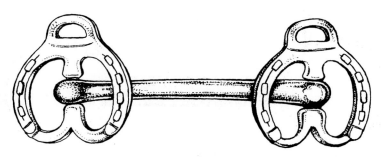

Stallion horseshoe cheek

Wire ring, wooden mouth breaking bit with keys

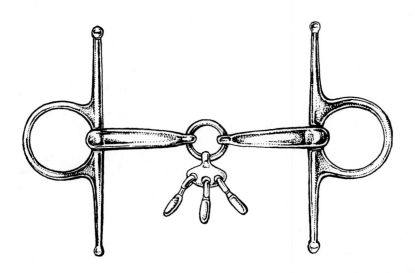

Full cheek single-jointed breaking bit with keys

94

INDEX

Above the bit 68
American gag 46, 47, 91
American Grakle 56
Aurigan 33
Australian cheeker 52, 59, 60, 69, 72, 74

Bars (of the mouth) 16, 17, 22, 23, 32
47, 50, 65
behind the bit 69
Belgian snaffle *see* Continental snaffle
bib martingale *see* martingale
bitguard(s) 20, 21, 36, 37, 39, 41, 54,
59, 66
bolting 69
bradoon 20, 21, 35, 39, 44, 75

Cavesson 54, 61
cavesson noseband 45, 52, 54, 56, 61
chain-mouth snaffle 47
cheekpiece(s) 9, 18, 19, 20, 21, 23, 27, 29,
32, 34, 35, 39, 40, 42, 43, 44, 46, 50, 56
cherry roller 31, 74, 88
cinch cavesson *see* doubleback
conformation 15, 26, 70
– of the mouth 9
Continental snaffle 46 *see also* three-ring
copper 25, 32, 33, 74, 79, 84
copper alloys 33
copper roller(s) 31, 33, 88
Cornish snaffle *see* Scorrier
curb 12, 20–2, 24, 45–7, 57, 61, 65–6
Cyprium 3

Dexter 41, 83
Dick Christian 30, 85
doubleback 53
double bridle 57, 61, 66
double-jointed 18, 21, 27– 30, 39, 84–7
Dr Bristol 30, 41, 86
draw reins 66, 69, 70
drop noseband 40, 45, 54, 57, 61, 68

Eggbutt 9, 20–1, 35, 39, 40, 42, 44, 63,
66, 69, 74, 77, 81, 82, 84, 86

Filet Baucher 39
Fillis 39, 40, 74, 86
fitting (a snaffle) 16, 18, 50, 66, 67, 69
Flash 52, 54, 56, 57, 61, 69
flat ring 35, 39
French link 17, 29, 30, 39, 47, 68, 69,
74, 75, 84, 85, 91
full cheek 20, 29, 34, 35, 40, 41, 42, 44,
54, 56, 62, 66, 69, 73, 77, 82, 85, 88, 94
Fulmer 29, 40, 54, 56, 62, 66, 69, 73 81

Gag (snaffles) 43, 44, 45, 46, 47, 65, 66,
89, 90, 91
German silver 33
Grakle 52, 54, 56, 57, 70, 72

Half-moon 27, 30, 34. 37, 49
half-spoon cheek 41, 78, 82, 87
hanging cheek 21
hanging snaffle 23, 39, 40, 74, 82
Happy Mouth 17, 34, 47, 49, 69, 76, 90

John Patterson bits 18

Kangaroo 33
keepers 29, 40, 41, 62, 73
Kineton 52, 57, 58, 72
KK 17, 28, 30, 31, 73, 78, 86

Lean(ing) on the bit 10, 20, 34, 70, 71
lever snaffle(s) 43, 46, 66
lips 12, 16, 18, 19, 20, 28, 36, 41, 48,
50
long-reining 65
loose-ring 18, 20–1, 23, 30, 34–7, 40, 44,
47, 54, 59, 66, 68, 70, 75–6, 78– 81, 84
lunge(ing) 65, 66, 68, 69

Magenis 31, 88
Market Harborough 64-5, 73
martingale 9, 22, 61-3, 65
- bib 62
- running 61, 63
- standing 45, 61, 62, 71
measuring (a snaffle) 18, 19, 35, 36
mouth 9, 11-13, 15-35, 37, 39-40,
    42-3, 45, 49-54, 57, 59, 60, 63-66,
    68-70, 73
mouthing bit 30, 31
mouthpiece 9, 11, 15-21, 24, 26-37,
    39-43, 45, 47-51, 58, 69, 70, 73, 74
mullen mouth(ed) 18, 25-8, 57, 66,
    69, 73, 77, 78

Nathe 17, 34, 47, 49, 69, 78
Newmarket bridle 39, 58-9
nickel 32, 33
noseband 9, 12, 22, 40, 45, 50, 52-4,
    56-8, 60, 61, 68

On the bit 10, 12, 20, 24, 34, 61

Pelham 24, 25, 26, 34, 39, 46
plastic 34, 43
port 30, 74, 78
Puckle see Kineton
pull (horses who) 10, 16, 25, 28, 42,
    43, 57, 59, 65, 70, 71, 72

Racing-snaffles 30, 36, 44, 80, 83
rearing 48, 71
rollers 27, 31, 33, 45, 70, 71, 72
rubber 20, 21, 28, 33, 36, 37, 39, 41,
    45, 47, 59, 62, 66, 74, 76, 78, 83, 88
running martingale see martingale
running reins 64, 66

Schooling problems 35, 66
Scorrier 37-9, 80
setting the jaw 69
side reins 66, 68

single-jointed (bits) 17, 21, 27-30, 39, 45,
    47, 49, 68, 69, 73, 79-83, 88-90, 94
size
- of bits 11, 18-20, 29, 35, 54, 73
- of horse's mouth 16-17
snaffle action 22
spoon cheek 41
Sprenger 33
stainless steel 25, 32, 33, 57, 77
standing martingale see martingale
straight bar 27, 28, 33, 34, 57, 76, 77
strong 12, 28, 30, 31, 32, 33, 34, 37, 69,
    71, 73

Teeth 11, 13-15, 19, 34, 40, 41, 49, 50, 73
three-ring 46, 47, 68, 72, 90 see also
Continental snaffle
tongue 15- 17, 18, 27-31, 33, 34, 39, 40,
    42, 47, 49, 50, 74
- evasions 18, 28, 40, 42, 49, 60, 73
- grids 74
- ports 74
- pressure 17, 28, 30, 74
training aid(s) 9, 64, 68
twisted snaffle 47, 92

Vulcanised 29, 34, 37
vulcanite 26, 76, 77

Waterford 31, 87
Weymouth 21
Wilson 37-8, 80
W-mouth snaffle 47
wolf teeth 14

Young horses 14, 28, 30, 74